GUIDE
TO THE
READING
TUTORIAL
CENTER

Louise R. Giddings

UNIVERSITY
PRESS OF
AMERICA

Lanham • New York • London

Copyright © 1989 by

University Press of America,® Inc.

4720 Boston Way
Lanham, MD 20706

3 Henrietta Street
London WC2E 8LU England

British Cataloging in Publication Information Available

Library of Congress Cataloging-in-Publication Data

Giddings, Louise R., 1939–
Guide to the reading tutorial center / Louise R. Giddings.
p.   cm.
Includes bibliographies and index.
1. Individualized reading instruction.   2. Tutors and tutoring.
3. College–school cooperation.   I. Title.
LB1050.38.G54   1989   372.4'147—dc20   89–30484 CIP

ISBN 0–8191–7513–7

To my son,

Gordon

ACKNOWLEDGEMENT

My most sincere appreciation is expressed to my husband, Dr. Morsley G. Giddings, for technical assistance, proofreading, encouragement, and continuous support throughout the development of this project.

TABLE OF CONTENTS

**DEVELOPING COMPREHENSION
SKILLS**

**ASSESSMENT OF STUDENTS IN THE
TUTORIAL CENTER**

PREFACE

This book is designed to assist education students and others who tutor children in reading. In the text, the tutor will find information on planning for tutoring sessions, using appropriate instructional materials, and on developing and assessing reading skills. The ideas presented here are intended to help make the tutoring experience a positive one for both the tutor and the student.

Individuals enrolled in tutorial programs have varying needs and abilities. In using this book, tutors may want to adapt ideas and suggestions to the needs of their own teaching situations. The book is a convenient reference - a handy guide. However, it should be used with creativity and imagination.

The author wishes reading tutors the very best in their work with students.

Louise R. Giddings

CHAPTER 1

THE READING TUTORIAL CENTER:
A CONCEPT FOR COLLEGE/SCHOOL
COLLABORATION

The reading tutorial center is an arrangement for college-school collaboration. More specifically, it is a learning environment where children and youth at a school site are given reading instruction by college students enrolled in reading methods courses. The tutorial center provides a practicum for the college students and it supplies the experiential base essential for the understanding and utilization of concepts and ideas presented in methods courses.

Field components of reading methods courses may be organized in various ways. Yet, the common goal of all field work is to assist individuals in teacher preparation programs in developing skills for teaching reading. *Becoming a Nation of Readers* (1985), the report of the Commission on Reading, states that prospective elementary school teachers should have more extensive preparation in teaching reading. Moreover, the report advocates that there should be stronger training in the practical aspects of teaching. Colleges are not simply encouraged, but challenged to develop ways of strengthening reading methods programs through the integration of practice with theory. Tutoring is one way that students in teacher preparation programs can develop skills for teaching reading.

Arrangements for tutoring children by college students may take different forms. In one program, for example, each student enrolled in a teacher education course tutored one fifth or sixth grade student from a selected public school. Each child then tutored a third grader on the lesson taught by the college student. The fifth and third grade students were often selected because they had similar reading problems, and the college student planned lessons to benefit both children (Thelen, 1975). In a program supervised by the author, college students in a reading methods course were required to spend at least one hour per week as volunteer reading tutors in the School Volunteer Program of New York City. Students were assigned to assist teachers in after school reading programs conducted by the New York City Board of Education. The college students tutored children under the supervision and guidance of the New York City public school teachers.

Regardless of the nature of specific programs, formats for tutoring by college students usually take one of three forms. First, small groups of children with common needs may be placed with a college student in tutoring sessions. This arrangement not only assists children with specific learning needs, it also fosters positive interaction among the group members. Second, in regular classroom situations, tutors can aid children in interpreting teacher-directed lessons and activities. The third and most prevalent form is individual tutoring that provides for specific, focused instruction and personalized attention (Sakiey, 1980). The present tutoring arrangement, the tutorial center, allows for individual as well as small group tutoring.

The tutorial center provides an opportunity for college students to instruct children in reading; it also has the purpose of presenting an environment that invites and encourages learning, thinking, and exploration. The environment must be established in part by attractive, thought provoking learning stations created by each tutor. From an affective point of view, the environment should be developed through attitudes on the part of tutors and supervisory personnel that show respect for the students and confidence their ability to achieve.

2

The concept of the tutorial center is applicable where college students take children from classrooms during school hours and work with them in specially designated areas in the school building. Even greater use of the center idea can be made where college students meet children in after-school arrangements in school sites. In the latter case, the center and its programs are given general supervision by the college instructor.

The tutorial center must involve joint planning by the college and the school system or district. The college is responsible for the general organization of the center and for the training and supervision of tutors. The school system must provide the facility, students, and other pertinent resources. Furthermore, the school must encourage teacher and parent cooperation. Both the college and the school can provide materials for the tutoring program. With mutual support, all parties involved can benefit from the collaboration. The major benefactors, however, are the college students and the children. The college students who must experiment in a microcosmic learning situation are challenged to create learning activities and pedagogical principles. On the other hand, the children are motivated to learn, and they are assisted in their reading growth and development.

Training of Tutors

Thousands of young people in today's society are in need of reading assistance. The extent of the deficiencies in reading is evidenced by special reading programs, reading clinics, tutorials and numerous programs funded by federal grants such as Right To Read and the National Reading Program. Because of time constraints, classroom teachers are often limited in their ability to give needed special attention to students. Tutoring by trained individuals can benefit many children.

3

Unlike many school reading tutors, students from teacher preparation programs have the advantage of being enrolled in course work which gives them background for the tutorial assignment. The following list of major topics from one college textbook, *Teaching Reading in Today's Elementary Schools* (Burns, Roe, and Ross, 1988), is representative of topics discussed in basic reading methods courses:

1. The Reading Act

2. Prereading Experiences for Children

3. Word Recognition

4. Meaning Vocabulary

5. Comprehension

6. Major Approaches to Reading Instruction

7. Reading/Study Skills

8. Reading in the Content Areas

9. Literary Appreciation and Recreational Reading

10. Assessment of Pupil Progress

College students, like other tutors, require special training for the tutorial service. They need support for the teaching situations in which they are placed. In preparing individuals for tutoring, at least two pre-service sessions are needed. The sessions might discuss information related to:

1. establishing rapport with students

2. obtaining information, advice and materials

4

3. applying informal
   diagnostic techniques

4. charting students'
   progress and keeping other
   records

5. developing motivational
   techniques

6. using specific materials

Topics appropriate for training sessions are discussed in *Developing A Successful Tutoring Program* (Koskinen and Wilson, 1982.) In addition to preservice programs, however, tutors need continued opportunities to share their experiences, to talk about their problems, and to seek guidance.

Support should also be offered by providing a tutorial handbook to the student tutors. The handbook, which can serve as an on-going reference during the tutorial period, should offer suggestions for working with children, developing activities, and using materials in reading instruction. This book is intended to serve such a function. Other useful texts have been developed by Koskinen and Wilson (1982) and Rauch and Sanacore (1985).

In summary, reading tutors do require training. Reading methods courses that run concurrently with tutorial services give tutors professional background and insight. With limited time in seminar and lecture sessions, however, many practical issues which students have to deal with in tutoring may be neglected. Special orientation sessions and tutoring handbooks can be of value to students. In addition, college instructors and school supervisory personnel must allow time to meet with tutors in order to discuss problems and issues that need attention.

Basic Principles for the Tutor

The following principles should serve as guidelines for reading tutors. They are ideas which must permeate all aspects of tutoring in the reading tutorial center.

The tutor understands and respects children. In the relationship between a tutor and student, the student must be relaxed and secure enough to devote his or her emotional, physical, and intellectual energies to the learning task. In order to feel this way, the student must be assured that the tutor is open, empathetic, and respectful toward him or her. Without the proper affective tone, it is difficult for effective teaching to take place. Educators have pointed out that the initiation of learning rests not on teaching skills, scholarship, and curriculum planning, although each is important. The facilitation of significant learning rests upon qualities that exist in the personal relationship between the teacher and the student (Rich, 1985).

The tutor strives to help students achieve success in reading. Many students in reading tutorials have been frustrated in previous attempts to improve their reading skills. It is for this reason that they have been chosen for tutoring. These individuals need to feel that the tutorial center offers them a new chance to learn and to feel good about themselves. The tutor should, therefore, build on students' strengths and interests in designing lessons and activities. In addition, the tutor should give positive reinforcement and encouragement to students in all reading endeavors.

The tutor is flexible in his or her approach to teaching reading. The procedures used by the tutor must take into account the needs, interests and abilities of the students. Tutors can use desirable aspects of a number of different methods for reading instruction rather than adhere to a single one. Programmed instruction, a directed reading activity, the language experience approach, a thematic approach, and free reading from self-selected trade books may all be useful at on time or another in the tutorial center. Tutors must always seek the best ways for dealing with their unique situations. Learning to read is a very complex process and many different factors are involved. Therefore, there is no one best method or procedure for all individuals.

The tutor builds upon the experiential backgrounds of students. The key to success is teaching is to utilize what students already know. As Brown (1986) points out, when previous learnings are used effectively, students can best learn whatever teachers choose to teach them. The tutor must capitalize on the backgrounds of students in creating interest and motivation for lessons and in building bridges between old and new ideas. At times, the tutor may need to provide experiences for the development of background for a particular learning.

The tutor brings novelty to reading instruction. The usual textbooks and workbooks in reading are sometimes symbols of failure, boredom, or frustration to students in tutorials. These students may respond more readily to new materials and new ideas. The tutor should seek ways to keep reading lessons fresh and alive. In bringing novelty to reading lessons, it is probable that newspapers, tradebooks, language experience stories, magazines, and games may often supplement, if not replace, more conventional reading materials.

Conclusions

Calls for tutors in reading are constantly being heard form schools, community groups, and organizations such as the School Volunteer Program, Inc. Usually, the basic requirement asked of those willing to devote time and energy to working with children is the possession of a high school diploma or equivalent

7

certificate. Admittedly, the personal attention which a child receives from an adult in the tutoring situation is in and of itself most valuable. Simply having someone show such interest in a child may be reason enough to assign a tutor to a young person. However, if improvement in the reading skills of children is the primary goal of the tutoring experience, then educators need to provide training to assist tutors in their service.

Students in teacher preparation programs, particularly those enrolled in reading methods courses, can be considered one group with a decided advantage in terms of tutoring assignments. The reading tutorial idea discussed in this book presents a format for involving college students in reading tutorials for children and youth. The arrangement serves not only to supply needed tutorial services to the schools, it provides the college students with the practical training needed to develop teaching skills. It is suggested, therefore, that the reading tutorial center concept be explored as much as possible in college/school collaborations.

BIBLIOGRAPHY

Chapter 1

Anderson, Richard C. *et al. Becoming A Nation of Readers.* Washington, D.C.: The National Institute of Education, 1985.

Brown, Thomas J. *Teaching Minorities More Effectively: A Model for Educators.* Lanham, MD: University Press of America, 1986.

Burns, Paul, Betty D. Roe and Elinor P. Ross. *Teaching Reading in Today's Elementary Schools.* 4th ed. Boston: Houghton Mifflin Co., 1988.

Ekwall, Eldon E. *Teacher's Handbook on Diagnosis and Remediation in Reading.* 2nd ed. Boston: Allyn and Bacon, Inc. 1986.

Koskinen, Patricia and Robert M. Wilson. *Developing A Successful Tutoring Program.* New York: Teachers College Press, 1982.

Koskinen, Patricia and Robert M. Wilson. *Tutoring: A Guide to Success.* New York: Teachers College Press, 1982.

May, Frank B. *Reading as Communication.* Columbus, Ohio: Charles E. Merrill, 1982.

Phillips, Rene F. *Encyclopedic Guide for Professionals in Elementary Education.* Lanham, MD: University Press of America, 1986.

Pope, Lillie. *Guidelines for Teaching Children with Learning Problems.* New York: Book-Lab., Inc., 1982.

Rauch, Sidney and Joseph Sanacore. *Handbook for the Volunteer Tutor.* Newark, Delaware: International

Reading Association, 1985.

Rich, John M.   *Innovations in Education.*   4th ed.
    Boston: Allyn and Bacon, Inc.,   1985.

Steiner, Karen.   "Peer Tutoring in the Reading Class.:
    Journal of Reading,   vol. 21, No. 3 (December 1977),
    pp. 266-269.

Thelen, Herbert.   "Tutoring by Students."   In *Teaching
    Today.*   J.   Michael   Palardy   (ed.)   New   York:
    Macmillan Publishers, 1975.

CHAPTER 2

PLANNING FOR THE TUTORING SESSION

The planning of instruction is most important if tutoring sessions are to be orderly and productive. All teaching must begin with some type of planning. Knowing what they want to do and how they plan to go about doing it gives tutors confidence and a sense of direction. In this chapter, basic guidelines for setting objectives, planning lessons, and setting up learning stations are discussed. This section is designed to help tutors develop a framework for organizing learning experiences in the tutorial center.

Setting Objectives

Each session which a tutor conducts with a student should be guided by one or more instructional objectives. In other words, the tutor should have some intended outcomes clearly in mind for tutoring sessions. There are different ways in which objectives may be stated. However, it is most helpful when they are stated in such a way as to indicate observable behaviors (Jacobsen, et al., 1985). Therefore, it is recommended here that an objective be written with a performance component. Without some specific behavior established for a student to accomplish and without providing an opportunity for the student to perform, it may be difficult to assess what a tutoring session accomplishes. It is important that tutors decide what they want to do and formulate objectives for their sessions.

Thus, tutors should give attention to how they state the objectives for their lessons. In writing objectives, the tutor should give the learning task of the student, the conditions under which the student is to perform the task, and some indication of the acceptable standard of performance. This model for

11

writing instructional objectives is adapted from Mager (1962). The tutor, however, must begin with some overall aim for instructing the student. Then, one or more objectives based on the aim can be formulated. Examples of objectives based on the aims of tutors are given below.

1. Aim: For my student to know the difference between statements of fact and statements of opinion.

   Objective: After reading an editorial from a local newspaper, the student will underline two statements of fact and circle two statements of opinion.

2. Aim: For my student to show comprehension skills at the literal, interpretive, and evaluative levels.

   Objective: After silently reading the assigned story, the student will answer one literal question, one interpretive question, and one evaluative question based on the story.

3. Aim: For my student to show the ability to utilize context clues.

   Objective: Given the cloze passage, "The Bird's Nest," the student will correctly supply at least 80% of the missing words from the passage.

4. Aim: For my student to identify the sound represented by the consonant p in the initial position.

   Objective: By the end of the session, the student will be able to raise his pencil to identify all words which begin with the initial consonant p when listening to a list of words recited by the tutor.

In each of the above examples, a basic aim for a lesson is given. This aim is then translated into a very specific performance objective that allows the tutor to tell whether or not the student has mastered or achieved the desired end. Each performance objective states the behavior to be performed, for example, "write" or "underline". The objectives also give the conditions under which the student will perform, for example, "after silently reading the story" or "when listening to a list of words recited by the tutor." Finally, each objective indicates some performance standard - the student will give "two statements of fact" or "supply 80% of the missing words."

It should be noted that in order to be of benefit, the objectives that tutors construct must be based on the needs, interests and abilities of students. Some objectives may be derived from informal diagnosis; others may come from information found in curriculum guides. Recommendations of students' regular classroom teachers can also be a useful source for developing objectives. Moreover, the special interests of students indicated through inventories and discussions with students can at times be used in formulating objectives. Regardless of the source of objectives, it is important that tutors gain as much information as possible about their students and formulate worthwhile objectives to assist students in their reading growth and development.

Writing Lesson Plans

Once objectives have been established, plans for teaching students and helping them to achieve the stated objectives can be formulated. Each tutoring session should be viewed as a teaching session where one or more lessons are taught. Although formats for lesson plans may vary, the basic elements of a lesson plan include stating one or more objectives, indicating procedures to be followed in the development of the lesson, and giving an evaluation plan. The specific format offered for use in the tutorial center includes the following six components: aim, objectives, motivation, materials, procedures, and evaluation. Each of these components is discussed below.

Aim. In developing the aim, the tutor must ask the question "What is it that I want to accomplish in this lesson?" The aim may be to teach the student to identify the main idea of a paragraph, or it may be to help the student know the meaning of the prefix "un." Once the tutor has established his or her goal for a lesson, the remainder of the plan can follow.

Objectives. As explained previously, objectives should be stated clearly in terms of the desired performance of the student. The objectives serve to identify the end product of the instructional sequence and help to focus steps leading to the end product. Objectives help tutors assess performance because they state behaviors in specific terms.

Motivation. The motivation component is an important but frequently overlooked aspect in the development of a lesson. The tutor should attempt to gain the student's attention and to help the student develop interest in the topic of the lesson. Motivating a student for learning can be a challenging task and often calls for imagination on the part of the teacher. A tutor may build motivation for a lesson by asking a stimulating question, showing the student a picture or photograph, reciting a poem, telling a short story, or having the student recall a related experience. In preparation for reading an article related to the history of the automobile, a tutor might ask: "How many types of automobiles can you name?" The prior knowledge of content activated during the motivation is important to reading comprehension. Motivating the student for reading is an essential aspect of

14

instruction. Tutors need to be skillful and creative in developing this component of the lesson.

Procedures. The procedures component allows the tutor to indicate how he or she intends to develop the lesson with the student. In this section, the tutor has an opportunity to state questions to be posed to the student, information to be presented, and the manner in which materials will be utilized. The procedures section, in effect, consists of a set of directions or instructions on how to present the lesson.

Here is an excerpt from the procedures component of a lesson plan on homographs.

1. Show the student a sentence with the word *wind* in it referring to motion of the air and a sentence with *wind* meaning to turn or make revolve.

2. Ask the student to compare the sentences and the meanings of the words.

3. Repeat, showing sentences for *bow*, meaning a part of a weapon and *bow*, a tied ribbon.

4. Again, ask student to compare the sentences and the word meanings.

5. Have student provide a definition for homographs.

6. Ask the student to supply another example of homographs.

Materials. In this component, the tutor should list everything needed to teach the lesson and to facilitate the achievement of the objectives for the lesson. For example, charts, audio visual equipment, books, glue, tape, and any other items used may be considered part of the materials component. When materials are noted in the lesson plan, tutors have the opportunity to

15

prepare prior to beginning a lesson.

Evaluation. In this component of the lesson plan, the teacher determines how he or she will evaluate the student's learning. This process need not be difficult if the objectives of the lesson are written in behavioral terms and include some standards for performance. Consider the following objective:

After reading an informational book on reptiles, the student will understand the concept of reptiles so that when given a list of animals, he or she will circle all animals that are reptiles.

The evaluation for this objective would be as follows; A list of animals will be provided and the student will be required to circle all reptiles on the list. As can be seen form the example, the evaluation must be consistent with the objective. Evaluation provides feedback to tutors and students as to whether or not lessons have been effective.

Sample Lesson Plan 1

TOPIC: Silent *e* vowel generalization

AIM: To teach the vowel generalization for silent
            e.

OBJECTIVE: After participating in this session, the
                student will be able to:

                (1) State the silent *e* generalization.

                (2) In five instances, choose from a
                     group of words, the word containing
                     the silent *e* pattern to complete a
                     sentence.

MOTIVATION: Display a picture of each of the
                following: a rake, a bike, and a kite.
                Ask the student to spell each word.
                Give assistance if necessary. Tell the
                student that he will use these words
                along with some other words for this
                session. Tell the student to notice the
                words carefully because he will learn
                something new about the words.

MATERIALS: Pictures of each of the following: a
                bike, a rake, and a kite. Response
                cards on which are written the answers
                "long" and "short". Activity sheet with
                context clue sentences, Chart with
                silent *e* words.

PROCEDURES: 1. Display the chart of words –
                including bike, rake, kite, side,
                rode, use, cake, like and ice.

            2. Ask the student to pronounce the
                words.

            3. Ask questions such as the following

17

to call attention to the visual clues
to word attack:

a) How many vowels are in each word?

b) What is the last letter in each
word?

c) What letter gives the last sound
in the word bike?   Ask this
question for the other words in
the list.

d) What can you tell me about the
sound of e in each word?

4. Repeat each word. Ask the student to
listen for the vowel sound in each
word.

5. Ask the student to hold up the "long"
card if he hears a long vowel sound
and the "short" card if he hears a
short vowel sound.

6. Ask the student to tell how many
consonants there are between the two
vowels in each word.

7. Ask the student: Can you say
anything about words with two vowels
when one of the vowels is a final e?

8. Give the following exercise for
application of the silent e
generalization.

Activity Sheet

From the three choices given for each sentence below, choose the word that makes the most sense to complete the sentence.

1. I have a new fishing _____.
   (pond, pole, pull)

2. I can fly a _____.
   (kid, kit, kite)

3. I ___ some candy for the party.
   (made, mad, man)

4. Sue _____ all the cake.
   (an, ate, at)

5. Can you _____ me to school.
   (driven, drive, did)

EVALUATION: 1. The student will state the silent *e* vowel generalization.

2. On the activity sheet provided by the teacher, the student will correctly supply incomplete sentences with appropriate silent *e* words.

VERNON REGIONAL
JUNIOR COLLEGE LIBRARY

Sample Lesson Plan 2

TOPIC: Sequence

AIM: To teach the student to establish the proper sequence of ideas and events.

OBJECTIVES: By the end of this lesson, the student will be able to:

1. State four activities she does in the morning in proper sequence.

2. Given a picture doll story, cut the story into separate episodes and put the episodes into a meaningful sequential order.

MATERIALS: Scissors, paste, "Humpty-Dumpty" rhyme, picture episodes of "Humpty-Dumpty," mimeographed picture sequence stories, and student's notebook.

MOTIVATION: Recite the old nursery rhyme "Humpty, Dumpty". Discuss what happened to Humpty-Dumpty and show the pictures based on the rhyme.

PROCEDURES:

1. Explain that stories are written in a certain order. First things happen first, something else happens, and then something else. We would not put the end of a story first.

2. Relate the idea of putting things in the order in which they happened to Humpty-Dumpty. Illustrate by having the Humpty-Dumpty pictures placed in the proper sequence.

3. Give out mimeographed picture story

20

on morning activities.

4. Say: "Let's look at this sheet. First, we will talk about the pictures and then you will think about the sequence or order in which they belong. What do you see in the first picture? How do you know that?"

5. Discuss with the student the fact that there is a certain sequence or order in her morning activities. Explain to the student that she will cut out the pictures on the sheet and put them in the proper order to show how she goes about her own morning activities.

6. Give the child a pair of scissors and a jar of paste. Ask her to cut the pictures out and paste them in proper sequence into her notebook. Emphasize that each person has his or her own routine in the morning.

7. Ask the student to number the pictures in proper order when she has completed the pasting. Then, bring the book to me to relate the sequence of her morning activities and to label the pictures: Arise, Wash, Dress, and Eat.

8. (Summary) Ask "What did you learn today?" Things take place in a certain order or sequence and we should be able to place things which happen in their proper order.

FOLLOW-UP: Tell the student: "I have cut a story into three happenings. I would like you

21

to take the pictures home and paste them into your notebooks in the proper order or sequence. Number the proper order of the pictures and then label the pictures if you can. You may have to have someone help you with the labeling. Bring the assignment in with you at our next meeting.

EVALUATION: The student will be evaluated by:

1.   Her oral responses.

2.   The exercise completed on morning activities.

3.   The completion of the follow-up assignment.

Sample Lesson Plan 3

TOPIC: Rhyming Words

AIM: To introduce the student to rhyming words.

OBJECTIVES: By the end of this lesson, the student will be able to:

    (1)   Repeat pairs of rhyming words heard in a story.

    (2)   Match pictures of objects with rhyming names.

MATERIALS: Storybook - *A Book of Rhymes*, puppet, picture cards for the pocket of the puppet, activity sheet.

MOTIVATION: Show cover of book to student. Say: "Today we are going to read a story. The name of the book is - A *Book of Rhymes.*

PROCEDURE:

1.   Display the cover of the book and read the title.

2.   Read the first page of the text and stress the rhyming words.

3.   Explain that the names Jerry and Terry have similar sounds because the endings sound the same. Therefore, Jerry and Terry are rhyming words.

4.   Continue reading the book to the student.

5.   Emphasize the rhyming words as each page is read.

23

6. Display puppet, Ms. Crockett, as seen in the storybook. Have student put his hand into the puppet's magic pocket to take out a picture card.

7. Ask the student to match each picture card with the picture in the book with which it rhymes.

8. Turn the pages again from the beginning of the book and ask the student to repeat each pair of rhyming words.

9. Summarize the lesson by reviewing the idea of rhyming words and asking the student to give his own examples.

EVALUATION: The student will be given a sheet displaying pictures to be matched according to rhyming sounds. The pictures will include a jar, a can, a star, a fan, a bell, and a shell.

Activity Sheet

Draw lines to match rhyming pictures.

A

BOOK

OF

RHYMES

A Book of Rhymes

By

Louise R. Giddings

Jerry　　Terry

Here are two friends.

One is Jerry.

The other is Terry.

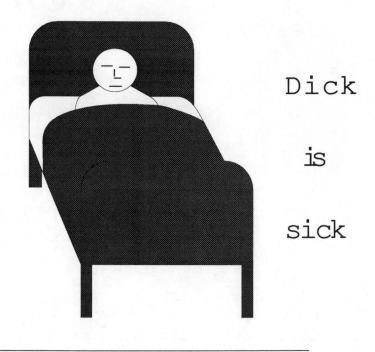

Dick

is

sick

The boys have a friend.

His name is Dick.

He does not feel well.

Today Dick is sick.

jar   car

Jerry has a little toy car.

He keeps it near the cookie jar.

hat   bat

Terry has a big black hat.

He also has a baseball bat.

30

Pat

Mat

Here is Jerry's sister Pat.

She is standing on a mat.

31

Ms. Crockett
has a

magic
pocket

Pat has a puppet named Ms. Crockett.

Ms. Crockett has a magic pocket.

star   moon   fish

Would you like to reach into Ms. Crockett's pocket
and take out a picture to match with one of the
rhyming pictures on this page?

In Ms. Crockett's magic pocket, there is something
that rhymes with star, something that rhymes with
moon, and something that rhymes with fish. Can
you find each rhyming picture?

And that is the end of the story.

How many rhyming words do you remember?

The

End

Sample Lesson Plan 4

TOPIC: Cause and Effect

AIM: To teach cause and effect relationships.

OBJECTIVES: After participating in this lesson, the student will be able to:

(1)   State what happens to certain story characters.

(2)   State why things happen to certain characters.

(3)   Identify and know that what happens is the effect and why it happens is the cause.

MATERIALS: The storybook of Little Red Riding Hood, activity sheets, chart paper.

MOTIVATION: Write the following questions on chart paper and ask the student to respond to them.

1.   What could be the effect if you ran across a busy street?

2.   What could be the cause of a baby crying?

Elicit the reason behind the student's answers. Tell the student that what he has just done is to give examples of cause and effect.

PROCEDURES: 1.   Read the story of Little Red Riding Hood to the student.

2.   Write the following questions on the chart paper and ask the student

35

to underline the cause and circle
the effect.

A.   Red Riding Hood's mother asked
her to take fruits to her
grandmother because she was
sick.

B.   The wolf asked her where she
was going because he wanted to
follow her.

C.   After seeing his big eyes she
was afraid.

D.   The woodman scared the wolf
and he ran away.

E.   Her grandmother let the wolf
in because he changed his
voice.

3.   Ask the student to write two
sentences of his own each including
a cause and effect relationship.

4.   Ask the student to read his
sentences aloud stating the cause
and effect in each.

EVALUATION: The student will be evaluated by the
structure of the sentences written and
by the activity sheet where he will
identify cause and effect relationships.

Activity Sheet

In each sentence below, draw one line under the cause and two lines under the effect.

1. Laura shouted at her brother because he made he fall.

2. Because it was a special occasion, June stayed up late.

3. Being very tired, Jody's eyelids drooped.

4. The pot was too hot, so Carl dropped it.

5. Peter was given an award for his great achievements.

6. Due to a severe headache, he was not alert in class.

7. Because of the grammatical errors, Jeffrey received a **C** on his English assignment.

8. I like David because he is a pleasant individual.

Various types of lessons may be planned for tutoring sessions. One lesson may be based on a passage from a textbook or a tradebook. Another lesson might involve learning a particular word recognition skill such as learning a few new sight words. Some lessons might focus on developing a comprehension skill, such as the ability to draw conclusions. Thematic studies in which students read, write and complete language related projects on a certain theme also make interesting lessons. Most tutoring sessions are set for approximately thirty to forty-five minutes. During this period of time, a tutor may teach one or more lessons. As Shohen (1985) points out, what a tutor does during a tutoring period depends on many factors. The most important factors to be considered, however, are the student's attitude, attention span, and specific needs.

Establishing the Learning Station

The station at which the tutor works with a student is usually no more than a table or an assigned portion of a table with chairs. Tutors must realize that the environment in which the student works can influence learning. Every effort should be made to make the learning station as comfortable, attractive, and intellectually stimulating as possible.

In order for the station to be comfortable, tables and chairs should be of an appropriate height and size for the student. There should be proper lighting so that there is no strain on the student's vision. The station should not be located too close to sources of hot or cold air such as heaters, ventilators, or open doors. Tutors should not be located too close to other tutoring stations. Such proximity can cause distractions and result in much wasted time during tutoring sessions.

Most importantly, tutors should make every attempt

to set up learning stations as centers for stimulating learning. Jackets of books may be displayed on tables; pictures or photographs may be placed on tables for motivation and discussion. Charts with vocabulary, statements, generalizations, questions to be answered, or with pockets for task cards may also be used. Charts may be components of games and other learning activities planned for a particular lesson. Well-planned learning environments can motivate and facilitate learning in the tutorial center. Each tutor must decide how to establish the environment in the station for each session.

Summary

Good teaching begins with planning. At times, a tutor may have to rearrange activities planned for a lesson or take advantage of unanticipated teaching opportunities. Generally, however, lessons and the learning environment should be purposefully and thoughtfully planned.

BIBLIOGRAPHY

Chapter 2

Burns, Paul, Betty D. Roe and Elinor P. Ross. *Teaching Reading in Today's Elementary Schools.* 4th ed. Boston: Houghton Mifflin Co., 1988.

Irwin, Judith W. and Isabel Baker. *Promoting Active Reading Comprehension Strategies.* Englewood Cliffs, N.J.: Prentice Hall, 1989.

Jacobsen, David, Paul Eggen, Donald Kauchak and Carole Dulaney. *Methods for Teaching: A Skills Approach.* 2nd ed. Columbus, Ohio: Charles E. Merrill, 1985.

Koshinen Patricia S. and Robert M. Wilson. *Tutoring: A Guide for Success.* New York: Teachers College Press, 1982.

Mager, Robert. *Preparing Instructional Objectives.* Palto Alto, Calif.: Fearon, 1962.

Shohen, Samuel S. "Basic Teaching Procedures" in *Handbook for the Volunteer Tutor.* Sidney J. Rauch and Joseph Sanacore (eds.). Newark, Delaware: International Reading Association, 1985.

Zintz, Miles V. *Corrective Reading.* 4th ed. Dubuque, Iowa: William C. Brown Co., 1981.

Chapter 3

USING MATERIALS IN THE READING TUTORIAL CENTER

Various types of materials should be available for use with students in the reading tutorial center. Adequate and appropriate materials are crucial to conducting effective tutoring sessions. Tutors, therefore, must become familiar with different types of reading materials and with how the materials can be used with students. The purpose of this chapter is to discuss some basic reading materials that tutors should use in their tutoring programs. The discussion includes basal readers, newspapers, language experience materials, and library books.

Basal Readers

Basal readers are commercially prepared reading texts intended to provide a comprehensive program for reading instruction. They are the most widely used materials for reading instruction in the schools of the United States (Spache and Spache, 1986). Although basal reading materials are published by many different publishing companies, these materials have some common basic features.

Basal reading programs are provided by most companies from the preprimer level through grade six. A few companies publish reading materials through grade eight. The student's reading textbook is only one component of a basal reading system. Most publishers provide workbooks and teacher's manuals.

Textbooks for students usually consist of stories and other reading selections. Workbooks are designed reinforcing skills that have been taught during reading lessons. The teacher's manuals contain facsimile pages of student textbooks. The manuals have detailed plans

41

that help teachers present reading lessons to students. Besides the teacher's manual, student textbook and workbook, publishing companies offer supplementary materials to be used in conjunction with the basic materials. These materials include such items as unit tests, specific skills books, charts, and duplicating masters.

It is important to note that most basal readers are carefully graded and have controlled vocabularies. With vocabulary control, students are introduced to unfamiliar words in a systematic way. Basal readers also provide for systematic and sequential teaching of word recognition and comprehension skills. The order of presentation of reading skills throughout any graded series can usually be found on a scope and sequence chart in the teacher's manual.

The teaching strategy recommended for use with basal readers is called the Directed Reading Activity. The following steps are included in a Directed Reading Activity:

Motivation and development of background. In this part of the lesson, the teacher attempts to interest the student in the subject of the reading selection. The teacher also builds background for the story through discussion of vocabulary and ideas from the material to be read. For example, a teacher may ask a third grade student to name and describe two different kinds of apples in preparation for a story that deals with the history of a particular type of apple. In talking with a fourth grader preceding the reading of a story of a boy who ran in a track meet, the teacher may wish to help the student develop an understanding of terms such as heat, meet, spiked shoes, starter and standing start. Tutors should try to activate a student's prior knowledge concerning a topic during the pre-reading period and help the student to build needed background knowledge. Recent research stresses the importance of prior knowledge to comprehension (Irwin and Baker, 1989).

Guided silent reading. It is recommended that the student first read a new selection silently. Silent reading allows for deeper concentration, greater speed in reading, and more opportunities to become independent in word attack skills than does oral reading (Durkin, 1983). The teacher should ask questions before a selection is read in order to direct and give a purpose to the reading. Later, there may be some oral reading of the story in whole or part to answer questions, develop expressive skills, and demonstrate word recognition techniques.

Discussion. In this part of the lesson, the student has an opportunity to discuss answers to the pre-silent reading questions, raise questions, and respond to additional questions. During the discussion, teachers are able to focus on the student's comprehension skills by asking various types of questions. Questions which involve literal, interpretive, and evaluative comprehension should be posed. Literal comprehension refers to acquiring ideas that are directly stated in a passage. Interpretive comprehension means being able to read between the lines and understand the implied meanings conveyed in written material. Evaluative comprehension requires critical reading. Such reading involves analyzing and making judgments concerning the ideas presented in written text. Thoughtful questions on the part of the teacher can stimulate thinking and help a student to respond at various levels of cognition.

Follow-up activities. The follow-up to reading from the textbook involves direct instruction and/or practice in some word recognition or comprehension skill. A word recognition skill lesson may focus, for example, on learning certain suffixes. A comprehension follow-up may give additional practice in noting the sequence of events in passages. Activities may make use of teacher-prepared materials, language games, workbook exercises, and other commercially-prepared materials.

43

Enrichment activities. An enrichment activity is not essential to every Directed Reading Activity. Nevertheless, when used, it can extend story concepts and allow students to think and work beyond the boundaries of the original reading selection. The enrichment activity may involve music, art, drama, creative writing, or additional reading and research. It provides for creative and thoughful responses to ideas acquired from the reading lesson.

In summary, basal readers offer a viable and effective way of conducting a reading session and instructing a student in reading. The teacher's manual offers lesson plans and many helpful teaching suggestions. Tutors may wish to draw upon basal readers from time-to-time in conducting reading sessions. The Directed Reading Activity is a highly recommended instructional strategy that can be used with basal reader selections as well as with other reading selections.

The Newspaper

The newspaper with its accessibility, low cost and varied content offers excellent reading material for the tutorial program. Because of the nature and difficulty of the content, it is most appropriate for students above the primary grade levels.

With its timely information, the newspaper helps young people to become aware of their environments while providing a vehicle for reading skills instruction. With a little skill and imagination, tutors can design effective reading lessons using the newspaper.

Tutors may view the newspaper as a text for interesting reading and, as with other reading texts, a point of departure for teaching specific reading skills. The following lesson plans are offered to give tutors ideas as to how newspaper lessons might be developed. The plans deal with identifying the main idea and with using context clues.

TOPIC: The Main Idea

AIM: To teach the student to recognize the main idea of a paragraph.

OBJECTIVES: By the end of this lesson the student will:

1.   Write headlines for news stories from which the headlines for the stories have been removed.

2.   Identify stated main ideas in straight news stories and other appropriate news articles.

MATERIALS: Newspaper articles, pictures.

MOTIVATION: Show the student an interesting picture. Ask the student to study the picture and then to write a caption for it.

PROCEDURES: 1.   Ask the student to tell what a paragraph is.

2.   Discuss what main ideas are. Use newspaper paragraphs to illustrate main ideas.

3.   Have the student select and read a news article. Ask the student to tell what the article was all about and then write down the main idea of the article.

4.   Give the student assistance if necessary in stating the main idea.

5.   Present the student with an article

45

from which the headline has been removed. Have the student read the article and write a headline for it. Compare the student's headline with the original newspaper headline

EVALUATION:

1. The student will be asked to match news articles with appropriate headlines.

2. The student will be asked to read a news article and write down in one sentence what the main idea of the article is.

TOPIC: Using Context Clues

AIM: To give the student the opportunity to
           practice inferential thinking by using context
           clues to complete cloze exercises designed
           with the newspaper.

OBJECTIVES: By the end of this lesson, the student
           will:
           1.   Read an editorial with certain words
                deleted and fill in the blanks with
                words that make sense.

           2.   Discuss answers from the cloze
                technique activity and give reasons
                for selecting words given.

MATERIALS: Newspaper articles in which words have
           been deleted.

MOTIVATION: Give the student the following sentence
           orally. "Would you prefer an orange or an
           _____ with your lunch?" Ask the student
           to supply the missing fruit.

PROCEDURES:
           1.   Tell the student to supply missing
                words now in written context.

           2.   Have prepared two cloze exercises
                using newspaper editorials. The
                exercises will be prepared by leaving
                the initial and final sentences of
                each editorial intact with no more
                than 10% of the words deleted.

           3.   Give directions for completing the
                exercises.

           4.   Discuss the importance of utilizing
                context clues to complete the
                exercises.

47

5. Have the student complete and discuss one of the two exercises.

6. Give the second cloze exercise to the student to complete.

EVALUATION: The student will be evaluated by his or her performance on the second cloze exercise.

The following page shows a fictitious newspaper article that has been cut up into sections and disarranged. In addition, the headline has been removed from the article. The student is required to place the sections in proper sequence and to give the article a title. This activity, which could be used with many newspaper articles, engages the student in two very important comprehension skills:

1. Identifying the logical sequence of events in a story.

2. Identifying the central thought of the article in order to write an appropriate headline.

According to a preliminary investigation of the May 23 fire at the Garden Plaza apartments, 135 Tuffs Ave., Brown said, ''There seems to have been some problems with the workmanship and completeness of the fire-retardent gypsum board that lined the compactor.

Faulty workmanship on the lining of a trash compactor chute could have played a mojor role in spreading the fire that killed six persons in an East Village high rise, Fire Commissioner Eugene Brown reported yesterday.

In other testimony, Paul Smith, president of the Garden Plaza tenants' association, said that some tenants told him that when they called 114 at 6 a.m. on May 23 to report a fire in the building, they were told that calls had already been received about a fire at that location. This information contradicted Brown's testimony.

He said further that a special board of inquiry set up to investigate the fire will study the evidence further and issue a report in about a month.

49

The newspaper is a tremendous resource for reading instruction. With careful planning, tutors can utilize the newspaper to help students increase their reading proficiency. Hopefully, newspaper activities with students will lead not only to reading improvement, but lifelong newspaper reading habits as well.

Language Experience Materials

Language experience materials are reading materials derived from the experiences and language of students. They are based on the following premise:

What I can think about, I can talk about.
What I can say, I can write - or someone can write for me.
What I write, I can read.
I can read what I write, and what other people can write for me to read. (Allen, 1973, p. 158)

Language experience materials may take the form of individual or group composed experience stories recorded by the teacher, or they may be individual stories written by students. Such writings may deal with field trips, school activities, personal experiences, observations, or imaginative stories or poems. Language experience materials can create a wealth of reading materials for students. They are unique in that they capitalize on students' personal experiences and interests.

In helping a student to develop language experience stories, the tutor should:

1. Encourage the student to discuss an experience.

2. Interact with the student to elicit additional ideas or clarify thinking.

3. For a researched topic, encourage the student

to tell what was learned.

4. Help the student, through questioning, to select and organize ideas to the used in the story.

   Questions such as the following may be posed.

   a) What do you want to include in your story?

   b) What would be a good title for the story?

   c) How will you begin the story?

   d) What comes first? What comes next?

   e) How will you end the story?

5. If the student cannot write his or her own story, have the student dictate the story to you sentence by sentence. Say each word as you write it down. Make sure the student watches closely as you proceed. Help the student re-word sentences for better structure and grammar if necessary. If a student is capable of writing his or her own story, the tutor can be available for guidance and assistance.

6. Have the student read the completed story silently allowing repeated contact with his or her own words in written form. A student may also take this opportunity to make sure the story is well written in terms of both ideas and written language. If appropriate, a student may even illustrate the story at this time.

7. Use follow-up activities based on the story to help the student develop better reading and language skills. For example, you may wish to use a story for:

a) <u>teaching a word recognition skill</u>. (If the story contains a few contractions, it might lead to a lesson on contractions.)

b) <u>comprehension development</u>. (If a figure of speech is contained in the story, it would present an opportune time to teach about figurative language.)

Sample Language Experience Stories

The following story was developed with a small group of first and second grade children who had attended a birthday party at a skating rink.

Our Trip to the Skating Rink

We went skating at the skating rink and had a lot of fun there. There was an Easter bunny rolling on skates. Alan fell once or twice or three times. We went to a birthday party while we were at the skating rink but we didn't get cake. All of us got a few bruises but still had lots of fun.

The next story was written by a fourth grade student who was engaged in a social studies unit on the Middle Ages.

My Visit to a Castle

I was in a coach looking at the castle. It had white and brown brick walls. The guards were stiff and smiling. The guards grinned and opened the draw bridge.

Inside the castle gates were stables that had shiny white horses that looked like unicorns. The bakeshops smelled so delicious that I almost bought ten cookies!

When I saw the dungeon I decided not to be bad. The serfs had small huts. They were so small I felt bad for them.

I walked into the great hall. There were many pictures on the wall which were beautiful. The fireplace made me feel very cozy. The long table was like the lunchroom table but much more fancy.

In the morning my friend (whom I was visiting) Jana Lee, took me to the table and we ate bread and drank wine. I was very surprised Jana Lee drank wine. After breakfast we went hunting. I did not like it but I went anyway.

When we ate our big feast, we had entertainment. I'm going to do what the singer does when I grow up.

I loved my visit. I said good-by to Jana Lee. I left.

The following story was written by a fourth grade student who was in a computer class.

Are Machines Taking Man's Place?

I think that machines are taking man's place because if you program the computer he will clean up the room and mop the floor for you. A lot of people like to clean so this is maddening to them. That is why I think that robots take people's places in certain jobs.

My father does not think that machines take the place of man. There are certain boring jobs that man hates to do. People now have machines doing them. Also these machines break down so you need repairmen to fix them and people to operate them efficiently. This makes new jobs for man.

The last story was developed with a group of second grade children who had visited an ice cream factory.

Our Visit to the Ice Cream Factory

We went to the ice cream factory. We saw the big cooler that makes ice cream cold. We saw the ice cream sandwich machine. A man gave everybody an ice cream sandwich.

Library Books

It is important that students be exposed to reading experiences that promote reading enjoyment and literary appreciation. Good literature can help students to expand their imaginations, increase their awareness of language, and develop greater knowledge of themselves and others. The use of books available in school and public libraries is crucial to a good tutoring program.

The range of literature available for young people is very broad. Tutors may guide students in reading from fiction as well as non fiction materials. Fiction may include such works as myths, fables, folklore, fairytales, realistic stories, historical fiction, and tales of exploration and adventure. Non fiction reading material may include biography and informational books in science, social studies, and other subject areas. Through discussions with children and by administering interest inventories, tutors can assess their students' personal reading interests and capitalize on these interests when making reading materials available.

Literature may be used with a student in various ways. With shorter selections, a tutor may wish to use the Directed Reading Activity or some adaptation of the Directed Reading Activity. At other times, the tutor may have a student read a selection and then complete some type of skill development exercise in word recognition or comprehension. Generally, a follow-up activity is recommended when the student has completed reading a selection. The follow-up may take the form of a creative response to the selection, an assignment calling for further study of a topic, or simply a tutor-student conference.

In addition, the tutor may wish to read stories and poetry to the student from time to time. Reading to a student has many benefits. Among them are the presentation of a good language model, the stimulation of reading interests, and the provision of literary experiences that the student may not be able to acquire on his or her own. Koskinen and Wilson (1982) offer helpful tips to tutors for sharing library books with students.

Many references are available to help teachers select appropriate library books for students. Tutors may find the following guides helpful:

"Children's Choices" in October Issues (annually) of *The Reading Teacher*. Newark, Delaware: International Reading Association.

Gillespie, John T., and Christine B. Gilbert. *Best Books for Children: Preschool Through the Middle Grades*. 2nd. ed. New York: R.R. Bowker Co., 1981.

Winkel, Lois et al. *The Elementary School Library Collection: A Guide to Books and Other Media*. 15th ed. Williamsport, Pa.: Bro-Dart Foundation, 1986.

Zintz, Miles V. *Corrective Reading*. 4th ed. Dubuque, Iowa: William C. Brown, 1981, Appendix B.

Tutors should also be familiar with the listings of Newbery and Caldecott award winners in children's literature each year. These listings should be available in all children's libraries. The John Newbery Award is presented to the author whose book is selected as the year's most distinguished contribution to children's literature and the Randolph Caldecott medal is awarded for excellence in illustration.

Literature can vastly enrich any reading program. It can help children to develop an appreciation for reading. Tutors should use literature wisely so as not to diminish the joy young people may find in reading library books. Highly-structured lessons may cause negative reactions and responses. Because reading from textbooks often represents boredom, drudgery, frustration, and even failure to many students, tutors should make use of materials that create interest, build motivation, and bring enjoyment.

The following references may be helpful to tutors in using literature with students:

Chambers, Aidan. *Introducing Books to Children*. Boston, Mass.: The Horn Book, Inc., 1983.

Gillespie, Margaret C., and John W. Conner. *Creative Growth Through Literature for Children and Adolescents*. Columbus, Ohio: Charles E. Merrill, 1975.

Lamme, Linda L., (ed.) *Learning to Love Literature: Preschool Through Grade 3*. Urbana, Illinois: National Council of Teachers of English, 1981.

Paulin, Mary Ann. *Creative Uses of Children's Literature*. Hamden, Connecticut: Library Professional Publications, 1983.

Shapiro, Jon, editor. *Using Literature and Poetry Effectively*. Newark, Delaware: International Reading Association, 1979.

Sloan, Glelnna Davis. *The Child as Critic: Teaching Literature in the Elementary School*. 2nd ed. New York: Teachers College Press, 1984.

Tiedt, Iris M. *Exploring Books with Children*. Boston, Mass: Houghton Mifflin, 1972.

Summary

This chapter cites basic types of materials for reading instruction and discusses strategies for using these materials with students. It is recommended that tutors use a variety of materials rather than adhere to one single type. Students in the reading tutorial center need enrichment as well as basic skill development through the use of varied materials and approaches. The discussion on materials given here should lead tutors to a serious exploration of materials for use in the tutorial center.

BIBLIOGRAPHY

Chapter 3

Allen R.V. "The Language Experience Approach." In *Perspectives on Elementary Reading: Principles and Strategies of Teaching.* Robert Karlin, ed. New York: Harcourt Brace Jovanovich, 1973.

Aukerman, Robert C. *The Basal Reader Approach to Reading.* New York: John Wiley and Sons, 1981.

Burns, Paul C., and Betty L. Broman. *The Language Arts in Childhood Education.* 5th ed. Boston: Houghton Mifflin, 1983.

Cheyney, Arnold B. *Teaching Reading Skills Through the Newspaper.* Newark, Delaware: International Reading Association, 1984.

Degler, Lois S. "Using the Newspaper to Develop Reading Comprehension Skills." *Journal of Reading,* Vol. 21 (January 1978), pp. 339-342.

Durkin, Dolores. *Teaching Them to Read.* 4th ed., Boston: Allyn and Bacon, 1983.

Grabe, Nancy White, "Learning Experience and Basals." *The Reading Teacher.* Vol 34 (March 1981), pp. 710-711.

Heitzman, William. *The Newspaper in the Classroom.* Washington, D.C.: National Educational Association, 1979.

Irwin, Judith W. and Isabel Baker. *Promoting Active Reading Comprehension Strategies.* Englewood Cliffs, N.J.: Prentice Hall, 1989

Koeller, Shirley. "25 Years Advocating Children's

Literature in the Reading Program." *The Reading Teacher.* Vol. 34 (February 1981), pp. 592-595.

Koskinen, Patricia and Robert M. Wilson. *Developing A Successful Tutoring Program.* New York: Teachers College Press, 1982.

Smith, Richard J. and Thomas C. Barrett. *Teaching Reading in the Middle Grades.* 2nd ed. Reading, Mass.: Addison Wesley, 1979.

Spache, George D. and Evelyn B. Spache. *Reading in the Elementary School.* 5th ed. Boston: Allyn and Bacon, 1986.

Chapter 4

TEACHING WORD RECOGNITION SKILLS

This chapter contains definitions, rules, and suggestions for teaching word recognition skills. These skills include having a store of words that can be recognized immediately by sight and having skill in using phonics, structural analysis and context clues. Tutors should assist students in developing the different word recognition skills as these skills lead to greater independence in reading.

Sight Words

In teaching sight words, a tutor should show the word while pronouncing it. The word may be shown in isolation, paired with a picture, or presented in the context of a sentence or passage. Using context for presentations is preferable; it gives meaning to words presented. After the initial presentation of a word, the student needs ample practice in recognizing the word. Practice should be varied and interesting. Games, flash cards, phrase cards, story reading, picture dictionaries, labeling, and rexo activity sheets may be made available to the student for practice in recognizing sight words.

Lists of basic sight words may give tutors some indication of what words are used most frequently in reading materials and, therefore, would be most helpful to students. The *Ekwall Basic Sight Word List* is a very useful list. The most commonly used basic sight word list is the *Dolch Basic Sight Vocabulary*. Both lists are presented below.

Ekwall Basic Sight Word List

1. a	41. then	81. us
2. did	42. where	82. an
3. have	43. can	83. find
4. know	44. can	84. is
5. one	45. in	85. other
6. to	46. not	86. something
7. and	47. this	87. very
8. do	48. who	88. around
9. her	49. come	89. fly
10. like	50. has	90. jump
11. play	51. it	91. over
12. too	52. of	92. stop
13. are	53. three	93. want
14. down	54. will	94. as
15. here	55. oh	95. from
16. little	56. you	96. let
17. put	57. your	97. ran
18. two	58. about	98. take
19. away	59. call	99. was
20. eat	60. had	100. back
21. him	61. mother	101. funny
22. look	62. see	102. man
23. run	63. time	103. red
24. water	64. after	104. that
25. be	65. came	105. way
26. for	66. he	106. blue
27. his	67. now	107. give
28. make	68. she	108. may
29. said	69. tree	109. ride
30. we	70. all	110. them
31. big	71. could	111. went
32. get	72. help	112. by
33. house	73. old	113. green
34. my	74. so	114. me
35. the	75. up	115. sat
36. what	76. am	116. there
37. but	77. day	117. when
38. go	78. how	118. saw
39. I	79. on	119. they
40. no	80. some	120. would

121. yes	163. work	205. each
122. again	164. been	206. grow
123. boy	165. cry	207. made
124. fun	166. into	208. place
125. long	167. must	209. ten
126. or	168. rabbit	210. because
127. soon	169. these	211. end
128. well	170. yellow	212. hand
129. any	171. before	213. many
130. brown	172. dog	214. right
131. girl	173. just	215. thing
132. Mr.	174. name	216. best
133. out	175. read	217. enough
134. stand	176. think	218. hard
135. were	177. began	219. men
136. ask	178. door	220. round
137. buy	179. laugh	221. those
138. got	180. never	222. book
139. Mrs.	181. shall	223. even
140. please	182. thought	224. head
141. tell	183. better	225. near
142. white	184. far	226. say
143. at	185. light	227. together
144. children	186. new	228. both
145. high	187. side	229. every
146. more	188. took	230. hold
147. party	189. black	231. next
148. than	190. fast	232. school
149. why	191. night	233. told
150. ate	192. sleep	234. box
151. cold	193. under	235. eye
152. happy	194. father	236. home
153. morning	195. walk	237. once
154. pretty	196. five	238. should
155. thank	197. four	239. until
156. with	198. always	240. bring
157. ball	199. does	241. fall
158. color	200. going	242. hot
159. if	201. live	243. only
160. much	202. pick	244. show
161. pull	203. sure	245. wait
162. their	204. another	246. carry

247. first	265. last	283. most
248. hurt	266. still	284. such
249. open	267. wish	285. wash
250. sit	268. gave	286. people
251. warm	269. left	287. write
252. clean	270. year	288. present
253. found	271. dear	289. also
254. keep	272. seem	290. don't
255. our	273. today	291. draw
256. six	274. done	292. eight
257. which	275. seven	293. goes
258. cut	276. try	294. its
259. friend	277. drink	295. king
260. kind	278. sing	296. leave
261. own	279. turn	297. myself
262. start	280. off	298. upon
263. while	281. small	299. grand
264. full	282. use	

Reprinted by permission of Merrill Publishing Company
from: Ekwall, Eldon E., _Locating and Correcting
Reading Difficulties_ (4th ed.) Columbus, Ohio: Merrill
Publishing Company, 1985, pp. 205 - 206.

The Dolch Basic Sight Vocabulary

a	come	
about	could	had
after	cut	has
again		have
all	did	he
always	do	help
am	does	her
an	done	here
and	don't	him
any	down	his
are	draw	hold
around	drink	hot
as		how
ask	eat	hurt
at	eight	
ate	every	I
away		if
	fall	in
be	far	into
because	fast	is
been	find	it
before	first	its
best	five	
better	fly	jump
big	for	just
black	found	
blue	four	keep
both	from	kind
bring	full	know
brown	funny	
but	gave	laugh
buy	get	let
by	give	light
	go	like
call	goes	little
came	going	live
can	good	long
carry	got	look
clean	green	
cold	grow	made

65

make	run	two
many		
may	said	under
me	saw	up
much	say	upon
must	see	us
my	seven	use
myself	shall	
	she	very
never	show	
new	sing	walk
no	sit	want
not	six	warm
now	sleep	was
	small	wash
of	so	we
off	some	well
old	soon	went
on	start	were
once	stop	what
one		when
only	take	where
open	tell	which
or	ten	white
our	thank	who
out	that	why
over	the	will
own	their	wish
	them	with
pick	then	work
play	there	would
please	these	write
pretty	they	
pull	think	yellow
put	this	yes
	those	you
ran	three	your
read	to	
red	today	
ride	together	
right	too	
round	try	

66

Phonics

Phonics is the association of speech sounds with written symbols. Being able to apply phonics understandings to help decode written language can be very helpful to students. Effective use of phonics skills allows students to pronounce many unfamiliar words. Phonics, in conjunction with other word recognition skills, can provide independence in decoding so that students can place greater attention on comprehension. The following phonics concepts and generalizations are basic in teaching phonics and are ideas with which all tutors should be familiar.

Consonants

The discussion of consonants is divided into (a) single consonants, (b) consonant clusters, and (c) consonant digraphs.

Single Consonants. The letters of the alphabet other than the five major vowels (*a, e, i, o, u*) are called consonants. Although most consonants have a single sound, some do not. Most notable exceptions include variations in the sounds of *c, g,* and *s.* The letters *c* and *g* generally have soft sounds when followed by *e, i,* or *y* (*g*ypsy, *g*inger, *g*ists, *c*ycle, *c*ent and *c*ity). When followed by *o, a,* and *u,* they usually have hard sounds (*c*ake, *c*at, *c*up, *g*um, *g*ame, *g*o). There are exceptions such as *g*ive, *g*et, and *g*irl. The *s* produces many sounds. One may note the different sounds of *s* in each of the following words: *s*un, *s*ugar, ro*s*e, and mea*s*ure.

Tutors should introduce one new consonant sound at a time. It is recommended that consonant sounds be presented in words rather than in isolation. One sequence for teaching consonant sounds is: *s, d, m, t, h, p, f, c, r, l, b, n, g, w, k, j, v, y, z, q,* and *x* (Kornblau, 1977). In addition to being familiar with individual consonant sounds, students should be able to identify sounds of consonant blends and consonant digraphs.

Consonant clusters. Consonant clusters (or consonant blends) are composed of two or three adjacent consonant sounds blended together with each sound maintaining its own identity.

Examples of consonant clusters include:

bl - blue	sk - ski
br - breed	sl - sleep
cl - clear	sm - small
cr - crow	sn - snail
dr - draw	sp - spin
fl - flew	spr - spring
fr - friend	st - store
gl - glad	str - street
gr - grow	sw - swing
pl - play	tr - tree
pr - proud	tw - twin

Consonant digraphs. Consonant digraphs are composed of two adjacent consonant letters that represent a single speech sound. Some consonant digraphs represent sounds not associated with either of the component consonants. The following units are usually listed as consonant digraphs:

th - think, then

ph - telephone

gh - rough

ch - cheer, chef, chaos

ng - sting

Vowels

The discussion of vowels is divided into (a) single vowels, (b) vowel diagraphs, (c) diphthongs, (d) r-controlled vowels, and (e) the schwa.

Single Vowels. The letters *a, e, i, o,* and *u* are symbols for the vowel sounds.

W and *y* represent vowels when they are in the final position in a word. The letter *y* also has the characteristics of a vowel in the middle position in a syllable or word. Vowel sounds are commonly classified as long or short.

The long vowel sound is heard when the sound is the same as the letter name. Long vowel sounds are represented in the following words:

*a*gent	g*a*me
*e*go	sh*ee*p
I	w*i*de
*o*dor	r*o*ll
*u*se	c*u*be

The short vowel sounds are represented by the vowel sounds in the words below:

*a*sk	s*a*t

egg   fed

it   quit

opera   sock

us   pup

   The symbol that represents the long vowel is called
the macron (-), e.g. ice. The short vowel sound is
indicated by the breve (˘), e.g. at. These symbols are
called diacritical marks.

   Vowel digraphs. Vowel digraphs are units of two
successive vowel letters that produce a single sound.
Some vowel digraphs represent sounds not associated
with either of the letters involved. Examples include:

        aw - saw

        au - taught

        oo - took

        oo - food

Other vowel digraphs usually represent the sound of one
of the component parts. Examples of such digraphs are
found in the following words: rain, beach, boat,
break, and eek.

   Diphthongs. Diphthongs are vowel sounds which are
so closely blended that they can be treated as single
vowel units. The four common diphthongs are:

        oi - foil   ou - bound

        oy - toy   ow - cow.

Note that the letter combinations *ow* and *ou* do not always represent diphthongs. In the word l*ow*, *ow* is a digraph representing the long sound of *o*.

R - controlled vowels. A vowel followed by the letter *r* does not produce either the short or the long sound. Such vowels are referred to as *r*-controlled vowels. Examples of vowels affected by *r* are found in the following words: c*ar*, f*ir*, h*er* f*ar*, g*ir*l, and f*or*k.

Schwa. The schwa is the soft "uh" or gruntlike sound usually heard in unaccented syllables. The sound is heard in the following words: *a*bove, funn*e*l, lem*o*n, circ*u*s, sof*a*, and butt*o*n.

Rules for Vowels

Some helpful rules concerning vowels are:

1.   In words which have two vowels, one of which is final *e*, the final *e* is usually silent and the first vowel is long. Examples include: d*i*me, r*a*ke, r*o*be, and c*u*te.

2.   When there is only one vowel in a word or syllable and it is followed by a consonant, the vowel is usually short. Examples are p*a*n, b*e*d, p*o*t, f*i*sh, and *a*lbum.

3.   When two vowels come together in a word, you usually hear the first vowel and the second vowel is silent. Singer (1982), however, points out that this rule has a limited utility rate.

72

Sample Activities for Reinforcing Lessons Related to Phonics

1. Have the student make a picture dictionary with pictures illustrating words beginning with each letter of the alphabet.

2. Play a game that requires the student to name other words with the same initial sound as a key word.

3. Have the student make a consonant blend book. Each page can have a blend accompanied by illustrative words and/or pictures.

4. Play word bingo.

5. Have the student read known sight words with a common consonant or vowel sound. Then have the student identify the common sound and the letter or letters which represent sound. The student can study word families in this manner also.

   (The tutor should add additional activities to this list.)

6._____

7._____

8._____

9._____

10._____

Structural Analysis

Structural analysis is another important word recognition technique. Skill in structural analysis allows the student to decode unfamiliar words by units larger than phonemes or individual speech sounds. Important elements in structural analysis include the identification of root words, prefixes, suffixes, compound words, contractions, and syllables. Students should be taught structural analysis understandings and should have opportunities to apply these understandings in practice exercises and in reading generally. Various aspects of structural analysis are discussed below.

Root Words

A root word is a word to which one or more affixes (prefix and/or suffix) may be added. The affix changes the meaning or use of the word. Root words are sometimes referred to as base words. Examples are: *continue* in dis*continuance*, and *happy* in un*happy*.

Prefixes

A prefix is a syllable added before a root word that changes the meaning of the root word. Examples are: *un* meaning not, as in *un*able; *re* meaning again, as in *re*read; and *multi* meaning many as in *multi*colored.

Suffixes

A suffix is a letter, letters, or a syllable placed after a root word to alter the meaning of the root word. Examples are: *ful* as in hope*ful*, *less* as in pain*less*, and *ous* as in joy*ous*.

Compound words

A compound word is made up of two words that have been joined together. Such words usually maintain the pronunciation of the two component words, and in the majority of instances, the meanings of the two words are connected to form the meaning of the new words. Examples of compound words are *snowman, cornbread, nowhere,* and *dishpan.*

Contradictions

A contraction is a shortened form of two words that have been joined together. In contractions, one or more letters have been left out and an apostrophe (') has been inserted instead. Examples of contractions are:

don't   (do not)

can't   (can not)

he's   (he is)

we're   (we are)

you'll   (you will)

let's   (let us)

Syllables

A syllable is a pronunciation unit which contains a single vowel sound. In general, a word has as many syllables as pronounced vowel sounds. The following words are divided into syllables: *be/gun, per/se/vere* and *e/go.*

Syllabication Principles

Tutors may wish to teach the following guidelines for dividing words into syllables:

1. Divide between a prefix or suffix and the remainder of the word. (Examples are *sub/way* and *hope/ful*).

2. When two consonants come between two sounded vowels, the division usually comes between the two consonants. (Examples are *tim/ber* and *win/dow*.)

3. A consonant which comes between two vowels is usually in the same syllable as the vowel following it. (Examples are *he/ro* and *ba/sin*.)

4. Consonant clusters and consonant digraphs function as single units. Therefore, they should not be split in syllabication. Examples are tea*ch*/er and ma/*ch*ine.)

Sample Activities for Reinforcing Lessons Related to Structural Analysis

1. Have the student underline or circle component parts of compound words.

2. Have the student identify original words from which contractions were formed.

3. Play "Word Ending Bingo." The bingo cards should have various word endings in the squares. The caller calls out root words from a prepared list. If a player has an ending that fits the word called, he or she covers it. As a check, a player must say the root words and appropriate endings from his or her card in order to win.

4. Make two word lists. See how many compound words the student can build by combining words from the first list with words from the second list.

5. Make a jig saw syllable puzzle game. Have the student put word parts together to complete the puzzle.

   (The tutor should add additional structural analysis activities to this list.)

6. _____

7. _____

8. _____

9. _____

10. _____

Context Clues

Context clues refer to the words, phrases, and sentences surrounding an unfamiliar word that help the reader to identify the word. The tutor should encourage the student to use context clues to figure out new words when possible. Context clues in combination with phonic analysis and structural analysis can give a student tremendous word recognition capability.

The following procedures can be useful in teaching students to utilize context clues.

1. Give oral sentences in which a word has been omitted and must be supplied by the student.

2. Give multiple-choice exercises in which you ask the student to identify the missing word to complete a sentence. For example: John ran to the (store, stop, see).

3. Introduce each new vocabulary word in a sentence context and allow the student an opportunity to say the word before pronouncing it for the student. This procedure is also suggested when the tutor listens to the student read orally.

In addition to the above, the tutor can encourage the student to utilize the following clues when reading:

Definition clues. In definition clues, the unfamiliar word is defined directly in the context.
Example: Tom wants to become a dentist. A dentist is a doctor who treats conditions of the teeth and gums.

Appositive clues. An appositive is a word or phrase, usually set off by commas, that restates or identifies the word it follows. As such, the appositive gives a synonym or description which may serve as a clue to

identifying a new word.
Example: The hue, or color, of the flower was violet.

Contrast clues. A contrast of an unfamiliar word to a familiar word may serve as a clue to the unknown word. <u>Example</u>: The house has not been abandoned for long. Last year people lived in it.

Comparison clues. A comparison of the unfamiliar word with a familiar one may also serve as a context clue. <u>Example</u>: Mary, who is usually late, was tardy again today.

Summary clues. In a summary clue, the unknown word sums up the ideas in preceding sentences. <u>Example</u>: First Johnny laughed at the clowns. Then he watched dogs jump through hoops. He also saw the elephants. Johnny had lots of fun at the *circus*.

Summary

Word recognition skills include phonic analysis, structural analysis, the sight word approach, and the use of context clues. The teaching of word recognition skills is an important facet of reading instruction. Skill in identifying words helps students to gain independence in decoding the printed page. With decoding skills, readers are free to focus on understanding and interacting with ideas conveyed in reading materials. In addition to developing their own plans and activities for teaching word recognition skills, tutors should make use of curriculum guides developed by school systems and publishers of reading materials.

BIBLIOGRAPHY

Chapter 4

Ceprano, Maria A. "A Review of Selected Research on Methods of Teaching Sight words." *The Reading Teacher.* Vol. 35 (December 1981), pp. 314-22.

Dallman, Martha, Roger L. Rouch, Lynette Y. Char, and John L. Deboer. *The Teaching of Reading.* 6th ed. Chicago, Ill: Holt, Rinehart and Winston, Inc., 1982.

Dechant, Emerald V. *Improving the Teaching of Reading.* 3rd. ed., Englewood Cliff, N.J.: Prentice-Hall, 1982.

Durkin, Dolores. *Teaching Them To Read.* 4th ed. Boston: Allyn and Bacon, Inc. 1983.

Heilman, Arthur W. *Phonics in Proper Perspective.* 5th ed. Columbus, Ohio: Charles E. Merrill Publishing Co., 1984.

Hull, Marion. *Phonics for the Teacher of Reading.* 5th ed. Columbus, Ohio: Merrill Publishing Co., 1989,

Jones, Linda L. "An Interactive View of Reading: Implications for the Classroom." *The Reading Teacher.* Vol. 35 (April 1982), pp. 775-6.

Kornblau, Esther. *Reading Handbook for School Volunteers.* New York: New York City Board of Education, 1977.

Lapp, Diane and James Flood. *Teaching Reading to Every Child.* 2nd ed. New York: MacMillan, 1983.

Olson, Joanne P. and Martha H. Dillner. *Learning to Teach Reading in the Elementary School: Utilizing a Competency Based Instructional System.* 2nd ed. New York: MacMillan, 1982.

Chapter 5

The essence of reading is understanding ideas conveyed in print. The development of word recognition skills is useful in that it helps free the reader to deal with the comprehension task. Once readers have facility in decoding words, attention can be focused on understanding and responding to written messages. This chapter deals with comprehension and suggest activities for helping students develop comprehension skills.

Vocabulary Development

An important phase in developing comprehension skills is the improvement of a student's vocabulary. A person can not understand what he or she is reading if he or she does not know the meaning of words in the passage. Developing a sight vocabulary has little value if word meanings are not understood. Some ideas for vocabulary development are discussed below.

1. Give opportunities for silent reading. Many, if not most, new words are learned either by hearing them or by reading them in context. As far as reading is concerned, Ekwall (1986) points out that after encountering a new word in context a number of times, the reader continues to verify a particular meaning that he or she believed was correct. One of the best ways of improving vocabulary, therefore, is to allow the student to have many opportunities for extended reading.

2. Have the student develop a word bank. Write each new word the student learns on a 3x5 card. Words can be kept in a shoebox. Periodically, review words with the student. Try various word bank activities such as:

   a) making sentences with words.

b)   categorizing words as nouns, action words, descriptive words, etc.

c)   finding words with common endings, roots, or prefixes.

3. Give exercises in which the student has to match words with definitions.

4. Use word games such as word bingo and tic-tac-toe.

5. Make use of commercial word games and vocabulary building activities.

6. Use crossword puzzles.

Teach the student what analogies are and give exercises with analogies. Analogies compare two similar relationships. An exercise may require the student to complete items such as the following:

a)   top is to bottom as up is to ____.

b)   mouse is to mice as coat is to ____.

c)   finger is to hand as toe is to ____.

It is important that tutors help students to identify relationships upon which analogies are built. Students may also be required to construct their own analogies.

7. Exercises with homophones, homographs, synonyms, and antonyms can assist in vocabulary development. Definitions and examples of these terms follow:

a)   Homophones - Homophones are words that are pronounced alike but are spelled differently and have different meanings. Homophones are enclosed in the parentheses for each sentence below.

84

Examples: I want to (*be, bee*) a fireman.

I (*hear, here*) a bell ringing.

b) Homographs - Homographs are words which have the same spellings but have different meanings. The pronunciations may or may not be the same.

Examples: I did not *wind* the clock.

I feel the wind blowing.

She has a *bow* in her hair.

You should *bow* before the queen.

c) Synonyms - Synonyms are words that have the same or very similar meanings.

Examples: The boy has a *big (large)* dog.

Susan was *unhappy (sad)* about leaving her friends.

d) Antonyms - Antonyms are two words that are opposite in meaning.

Examples: Antonyms for words in Column A may be found in Column B, *Happy* and *sad,* for example, are antonyms.

Column A	Column B
happy	strong
good	fat
weak	bad
thin	sad

8. Teach word origins. Latin and Greek roots are particularly helpful for students to learn. Note, for example, how the following words might be analyzed:

> *port* from the Latin *portare* means <u>to carry</u>

> *por*table - capable of being carried

> im*port* - carry in

> ex*port* - carry out

> trans*port* - carry across.

Important Comprehension Skills

A skilled reader uses various comprehension skills to understand and relate to information in printed material. Important comprehension skills and sample exercises for fostering the development of these skills are discussed below.

Noting Details

Noting details is the skill of recognizing basic information or factual data from a paragraph or passage. After a student has read a passage, the tutor may wish to pose questions to see if the student can recall bits of information conveyed by the material. Because detail questions are mainly concerned with information explicitly stated in a passage, they require little depth of comprehension. Such questions are usually of the who, what, when, and where variety. Detail questions are fairly easy to construct. Examples are:

a) Who was running down the street?

b)   Where did the story take place?

c)   At what time did Mary eat dinner?

Identifying the Main Idea

The main idea of a story or selection is the central theme around which the passage is built. The main idea of a paragraph is the central thought of the paragraph; it is the idea around which the entire paragraph is organized. The main idea of a paragraph is often, though not always, expressed in a topic sentence. The skill of recognizing the main idea involves reading to get at the core of the information. Details relate to the main idea by adding information to support the central thought.

A thought may raise questions or present exercises to help a student arrive at the main idea of a passage. The following suggestions may be helpful.

1. Ask the student to give a title to a paragraph or a selection.

2. Ask the student to express in his or her own words what the main idea of a paragraph is.

3. Offer a multiple choice exercise in which the student must select the appropriate statement of the main idea.

4. Have the student give a headline to a newspaper article in which the headline has been removed.

5. Have the student underline the main idea in a paragraph in which the main idea is stated.

6. Have the student write a paragraph with a topic sentence.

Identifying the Sequence

Skill in identifying the sequence of ideas means that the student is able to relate ideas from reading material in the proper order. A task such as the following would require a student to display knowledge of the sequence of events: Give, in correct order, four things Peter did when he heard the little girl call for help.

A tutor can help a student recognize the sequence of events and ideas by asking the student to:

1. Tell the steps to be followed in a procedure given in some reading material.

2. Give the chain of events in an historical reading.

3. Note words which signal time order such as now, before, after, while, yet, finally, another, and subsequently.

4. List the events leading to a scientific discovery.

5. Place in correct order, a newspaper article which has been cut in to sections and the sections disordered.

Making Inferences

The skill of making inferences involves what is known as reading between the lines. It is the process of arriving at ideas that are implied in a selection but not directly stated. In reading, a student may infer things such as:

1.   an unstated main idea

2.   conclusions

3.   the author's purpose

4. a character's feelings

5. reasons for a character's behavior

6. facts not explicitly stated

7. omitted words

Tutors should frequently pose questions that require inferential (or interpretive) thinking. Thinking at this level is more intellectually demanding for students than simply retrieving stated data. It is important that students be encouraged to respond to reading material at the inferential level and not to focus mainly on recalling factual information. The following example is illustrative of a reading passage followed by inferential questions.

> The brief snowfall had stopped. The fresh snow lay crisp and white on the ground. Mary looked out through her window and decided that it was now time to go out and complete her holiday shopping. She put on her boots, coat, hat, and mittens. Soon she was on her way.

1. What holiday is Mary preparing for?

2. What season of the year is it?

Students may be led to draw inferences by engaging in such activities as:

1. completing a story.

2. anticipating what will happen next in a story.

3. interpreting graphic data.

4. drawing conclusions from information given.

5. completing cloze exercises.

89

The use of cloze exercises can be very helpful in teaching inferential comprehension. In using the cloze procedure, a tutor should delete some of the words in a passage and have the student to fill in as he or she reads by inferring the missing words from the context clues. Gillet and Temple (1986) offer helpful suggestions for using the cloze procedure with students.

In constructing a cloze exercise, the tutor should leave the initial and final sentences of the passage intact and delete no more than 10 percent of the words. A passage of any length can be chosen and deletions can be made at random or at regular word intervals. If the tutor wishes to focus on a particular skill, however, he or she can leave out a particular part of speech, for example, pronouns. An example of a cloze passage may be found below.

You are learning new things all the time. Take ____ trip. Visit a zoo. ____ the newspaper . Talk ____ a doctor, policeman or bus ____ . All these things help you to ____ . School is not the only ____ where you learn new ____ . Learning takes place as you live and grow and have new experiences.

Evaluating Information

In evaluating reading material, an individual makes judgments concerning the accuracy and logic of the information. Such judgments depend upon more than the stated and inferred information offered by the author. They require the reader to have enough experience related to the situation involved to establish criteria or standards for comparison. An example of evaluative questions based on a story might be: Was Jim a good son? Why or why not? These questions challenge the reader to establish standards for being a good son and then to compare Jim's behaviors against the established standards. Then and only then can a judgment be made concerning the character's rating as a son.

Questions such as the following also require evaluative thinking.

1.   Is this historical account biased?

2.   Is this science book up-to-date?

3.   Does the author approach this material emotionally or logically?

4.   Why did the author write this material?

5.   Is the author qualified to write about this subject?

6.   Could this story really have happened?

7.   Are the characters in this story believable?

8.   Is this statement a fact or an opinion?

Being able to evaluate written material is critical to being a good reader. At the level of evaluation, a reader must be active and literate. The reader must question ideas, search for facts, and withhold judgments until all information has been carefully considered. Through questions and activities used, tutors should challenge students to engage in evaluative reading.

Sample Story with Comprehension Questions

The story below is followed by a list of comprehension questions. With the exception of one inferential question, the questions are general enough to be used with almost any story. Tutors may wish to adapt these questions for use with students in the tutorial center. Sometimes questions may be presented orally; at other times a tutor may wish to have a student respond in writing. It is important, however, that questions such as those presented here be complemented with more specific questions that challenge students to respond at the inferential, evaluative, and even creative levels of thinking.

Hector and Creepy

by Louise R. Giddings

One cool windy day in early October a mother grasshopper hopped to a small hole in the middle of a backyard garden, and there she laid her eggs. The days of fall past swiftly and then the cold winter weather touched the land. During this time the grasshopper eggs remained safe and alive in their little hole in the garden. It seemed as though winter would never end, but at last the winds grew warm. Tiny plant shoots began to project from the ground. Spring had come.

The grasshopper eggs, which had lain patiently in the garden throughout the long winter, also felt the warmth of spring. They knew that it was time for them to emerge from their eggs. Each day a brand new nymph, the name for a baby grasshopper, hatched from its egg. One day Hector, a fine strong nymph, broke through his shell and came out to greet the beautiful spring garden. Hector was greatly pleased with all the lovely green leaves he saw about him. He was also pleased to be able to move around the garden and feast on the plants.

Hector was quite proud of his beautiful green coat, his rather stubby jointed legs and his nice straight antennae that helped him to smell and touch the plants in the garden. He loved to munch on the green leaves, but looked a bit funny as his jaws moved from side to side as he ate. Each day was a new experience for Hector because there were so many new things to see in the garden and always many new plants to taste.

One day as Hector was moving about, he noticed something rather strange. A caterpillar, a round worm-like creature, broke out of an egg on a leaf of a flowering plant and began to inch its way along the leaf. Hector was amazed at the sight of the little animal. Its body was decorated in green, black, white,

93

and yellow, and it seemed to have several mini-legs and a segmented body which allowed it to move slowly along the plant stem. The creature never hopped about as Hector did, but appeared almost to cling to the plant on which it moved.

Hector's thoughts of pride began to take control. He could not resist comparing himself to the creeping creature which he immediately named Creepy. "My," he thought, "I'm glad I'm not a creeper. I can hop about this garden easily and I can go wherever I please. Besides, I can feel my wings developing, and when I molt, my wings will come out and I will surely be the most splendid animal in this garden. I will be strong and swift. What a pity to be a poor earth hugger like Creepy."

Although Hector had seen many other small animals run, hop, or fly around the garden, he found Creepy to be a most curious sight and often hopped near him just to stare. Once Hector almost laughed when Creepy nearly fell from a stem, but recovered his balance as he caught hold to a strong leaf and fixed himself there very firmly. Hector thought to himself, "What a pity to be such a clumsy worm. I would rather be a rock than to crawl about the earth like Creepy."

As the weeks passed Hector grew and grew. He became stronger and stronger. He did indeed become one of the most splendid animals in the garden. He felt great pride in his strength and beauty, and sometimes took pleasure in demonstrating his hopping skills as he often passed by Creepy who was usually inching his way along a stem or leaf looking for food. As Hector reveled in his own might and splendor, he often mused, "How Creepy must envy me. My legs are long and strong. My wings are sturdy and help me jump long distances. My long antennae guide me in deciding what is good to eat and where it is safe to travel. Perhaps, one day, I will become ruler of the garden kingdom. I will control all lowly creatures like Creepy and make them obey my commands. I will sit atop my throne on the

94

tallest bush in the garden and survey all my kingdom. Yes, I will become king and ruler of this garden."

Watching Creepy crawl along always gave Hector increased feelings of power and strength. But one day something very interesting happened. Hector watched as Creepy seemed to throw off his old coat of green, white, black and yellow, and allowed a new bigger body to emerge. Now, Hector had gone through a similar molting process himself, one which permitted him to grow in size and strength. Hector was not worried, however, that Creepy would ever grow to attain the splendor or beauty that he possessed. For, after all, Creepy was an earth crawler. Creepy was bound to the earth and could not hop or jump long distances as he could. No matter how large Creepy grew, he could only crawl along the plants and risk the chance of falling to a leaf or maybe worst, to the ground. No, Hector was sure that Creepy could not develop into a mighty creature as he was. Creepy could never become garden king.

Hector was almost dumbfounded, however, a week later when he saw Creepy attach himself to a twig by a silk thread and shed his skin to reveal a bright green cocoon. Hector could not believe his eyes as Creepy seemed to transform miraculously. The slow inching worm was now a still, motionless, suspended object. Creepy was gone.

At first Hector felt sad. "Poor Creepy," he thought, "I'll never see him again." Hector never thought that he would miss Creepy. He never really made friends with Creepy. He never talked to him or really wanted to know him. And now Creepy was gone. But then, Hector missed Creepy for another reason. No other animal in the garden seemed so lowly as Creepy. Creepy was an earth hugger. He seemed to struggle along through life so slowly and so clumsily. Looking at Creepy made Hector feel big and strong and powerful. Hector could not compare himself with anyone else and feel as royal as he did when Creepy was around. With

95

Creepy gone, Hector simply did not feel like a king. Hector searched throughout the garden looking for another creature who would make him feel like a king, but he found none. Yet, he put on daily hopping demonstrations and moved throughout the garden still hoping to recapture his pride and his place as king of the garden.

One day, Hector hopped by to take a look at Creepy's cocoon. Secretly, he was hoping that old Creepy would have broken out of his cocoon and that he would be crawling along a stalk. But, the cocoon was still there. Hector returned to the cocoon several times during the next few weeks, but no Creepy was to be seen. The odd shaped cocoon just hung from the stalk, calmly and quietly, as thought it would be there forever.

On one occasion, however, when Hector returned to look at the cocoon, he was frozen in amazement and wonder. A most glorious sight unfolded before his eyes. Beautiful colors of orange and black became visible in the cocoon. The colors seemed to be part of a moving web. Then as the web stretched itself out farther, Hector would tell that it was really a large, lovely wing. He could hardly believe his eyes. Pretty soon Hector could see that there were two wings in the cocoon. Then the most beautiful creature that Hector had never seen emerged from the cocoon. It was a butterfly, gloriously colored and more elegant and splendid than any animal in the garden.

Hector wondered, "Could this be Creepy? Could lowly earth hugging, stalk crawling Creepy be transformed into this majestic animal?" Hector wanted to speak to the butterfly. He wanted to know if it was the new Creepy. There were so many things he wanted to ask the butterfly, but he did not speak. He just stood watching in awe as the butterfly broke loose and freed himself completely from the cocoon. Then, the lovely creature flew away. Hector stood, watched as the butterfly departed, and whispered faintly, "Goodbye reepy."

Name_____ Grade_____ Age____

Teacher_____

Selection_____

1. Name an important character from the story.

   _____

2. List three important facts about the character you
   named above.

   a._____

   b._____

   c._____

3. Who is a very important person or character in the
   story other than the character you named above?

   _____

4. Why is the character you named in question 3
   important?

   _____

   _____

   _____

   _____

5. Where is the setting of the story?

   _____

6. How does the story end?

_____

_____

_____

7. List three major events from the story in the order
   they occurred.

   a._____

   _____

   b._____

   _____

   c._____

   _____

8. Is the title for this story a good one?

   a.   Yes_____   No_____

   b.   Why?_____

   _____

   c.   What other title might be good for this story?

   _____

   _____

9. Write three new words from this story.
   Use each new word in a sentence.

   <u>Word</u>   <u>Sentence</u>

a._____   a._____

                           _____

b._____   b._____

                           _____

c._____   c._____

                           _____

10. Do you think that Hector was sad to see the
    butterfly leave the garden? Why or Why not?

_____

_____

_____

Summary

Comprehension is the central factor in all reading. Vocabulary is an important aspect of reading comprehension. Instruction in vocabulary can help promote reading achievement. Tutoring in reading should include varied techniques and strategies to help students connect new terms to prior knowledge and make the new vocabulary a part of their basic language usage.

In addition, good comprehension depends on an individual's facility with various comprehension skills. Some important skills that student should master include the ability to note details, the ability to identify main ideas, the ability to identify the sequence of ideas, the ability to make inferences, and the ability to evaluate information. Tasks and activities that assist students in the development of comprehension skills are essential to all programs that seek to enhance reading achievement.

BIBLIOGRAPHY

Chapter 5

Burns, Paul C., Betty D. Roe, and Elinor P. Ross. *Teaching Reading in Today's Elementary Schools.* 4th ed. Boston: Houghton Mifflin, 1988.

Ekwall, Eldon. *Teacher's Handbook on Diagnosis and Remediation in Reading.* Boston: Allyn and Bacon, 1986.

Gillet, Jean W. and Charles Temple. *Understanding Reading Problems.* 2nd ed. Boston: Little Brown and Company, 1986.

Goodman, Yvetta M., Carolyn Burke, and Barry Sherman. *Reading Strategies: Focus on Comprehension.* New York: Holt, Rinehart and Winston, 1980.

Heilman, Arthur W., Timothy Blair, and William H. Rupley. *Principles and Practices of Teaching Reading.* 4th ed. Columbus Ohio: Charles E. Merrill, 1981.

Irwin, Judith and Isabel Baker. *Promoting Active Reading Comprehension Strategies.* Englewood Cliffs, N.J.: Prentice Hall, 1989.

Pope, Lillie. *Guidelines to Teaching Remedial Reading.* North Bergen, N.J.: Book-Lab, Inc., 1975.

Rauch, Sidney and Joseph Sanacore (eds.). *Handbook for the Volunteer Tutor.* 2nd ed. Newark, Delaware: International Reading Association, 1985.

Zintz, Miles V. and Zelda Maggart. *The Reading Process: The Teacher and the Learner.* 4th ed. Dubuque, Iowa: William C. Brown, 1984.

Chapter 6

ASSESSMENT OF STUDENTS IN THE TUTORIAL CENTER

Reading assessment is concerned with measuring achievement and collecting data on student performance. In order to address the needs of students and plan intelligently for tutoring sessions, tutors need to obtain as much information as possible about the skills and abilities of their students. The purpose of this chapter is to discuss ways of obtaining information about students' reading performance.

Background Information

Tutors need to ask: What is the background of my student? What has the student's past academic performance been like? What are some areas I might work on to be of help to the student. Answers to such questions can be obtained from teachers, school records, and from other sources. The following ideas can be helpful in seeking background information.

Consult the Student's Regular Classroom Teacher

Perhaps nothing is more valuable in obtaining information about a student than consulting with the regular classroom teacher. The classroom teacher has pertinent information concerning the student's physical, intellectual, and emotional development. It is logical that the tutor obtain needed information from the teacher rather than attempt to undertake any major assessment program during the short tutorial period.

The tutor may ask the teacher to supply information concerning:

103

A. General Student Behaviors

    1.   Classroom behavior

    2.   Reactions to authority

    3.   Attitude toward school

    4.   Attitude generally

    5.   Overall academic performance

    6.   Work and study habits

    7.   Ability to concentrate

B. Reading Development

    1.   Attitude toward reading

    2.   Sight vocabulary development

    3.   Ability to use context clues

    4.   Ability to use phonics

    5.   Ability to use appropriate reading rates

    6.   Ability to read with fluency

    7.   Any abnormal reading behaviors

    8.   Level of reading achievement

    9.   Grouping for reading

    10.   Reading materials used in class.

C. Physical Condition

    1.   Vision

2.   Hearing

3.   General Health

D. Emotional Adjustment

Obtain Results of Formal Reading Tests

Formal reading tests are commercially-prepared instruments. Some are norm-referenced in that they compare students with a representative sampling of other students. Others are criterion-referenced. These tests measure mastery of specific reading skills. The tutor should obtain test results from teachers or school administrators. In some instances, the tutor may be allowed to study the student's cumulative records to gather data. With such information, the tutor should note levels of achievement and dates on which tests were administered.

Most formal or standardized group reading tests used in the schools today are survey tests which give information relative to general reading achievement. They have limited diagnostic value. A tutor may not receive much insight form the scores as to specific types of word recognition or comprehension problems. It should be noted also that because most standardized group reading tests employ multiple choice answers, guessing is always a factor which can lead to misleading test results. However, the formal group tests do, in most cases, give the tutor a general picture of a student's reading capability. Representative group survey tests in reading include:

Test of Reading Comprehension (TORC).   PRO-ED, 1986.

This test assesses vocabulary and comprehension achievement.   (Grades 2-12)

Gates MacGinitie Reading Tests. Riverside Publishing Company, 1978.

This instrument tests vocabulary development and comprehension. (Grades 1-12)

Iowa Tests of Basic Skills. Riverside Publishing Company,

This instrument has subtests that focus on vocabulary, comprehension, and word analysis. For the primary levels, a listening test is also included. (Grades K-8)

California Achievement Tests. C and D (Reading). CTB/McGraw Hill, 1978.

These tests are in the areas of vocabulary and comprehension for grades K through 12.

Metropolitan Reading Tests. (Reading). The Psychological Corporation, 1978.

This is a comprehension test available for grades K through 12.

At times, individual survey tests may be administered to students. Some widely used individual survey tests include:

Wide Range Achievement Tests (WRAT). Stoelting, 1978.

The focus of WRAT is word attack skill. (Ages 5 - Adult)

Woodcock Reading Mastery Tests. Revised Edition. American Guidance Services, 1986.

The focus of these tests is on comprehension and word attack. (Grades K-12)

Diagnostic tests are also available in the area of reading. They are composed of various subtests that assess different components of reading. Diagnostic reading batteries are most comprehensive in the areas of readiness and word recognition skills. These tests are helpful in giving a profile of a remedial student. One highly recommended individualized diagnostic reading test is:

> *Durrell Analysis of Reading Difficulty.* Revised Edition. Psychological Corporation, 1980.

Informal Assessment Measures

Although information from formal measures may be available, it is necessary for tutors to do informal probes to gain further information and to develop new perspectives on their students. Moreover, informal assessment measures are needed for the on-going instructional process. They provide the means for noting strengths and weaknesses and for adjusting instruction to meet the needs of students.

The Informal Reading Inventory

One informal measure that can be most effective in furnishing tutors with crucial information about a student's reading ability is the informal reading inventory. The informal reading inventory is an individual measure of graded reading selections. The student is required to read the sequentially arranged selections until the material becomes too difficult. Throughout the test, the teacher makes notes of differences between the student's oral reading and the actual words in the text. The teacher also notes the student's answers to the comprehension questions posed by the teacher following the reading of each passage. The test provides a look at how the reader functions during the reading process. It allows the tutor to know the kinds of errors or miscues a student makes in oral reading and to gain insight into the student's comprehension skills.

The informal reading inventory can also provide the tutor with an estimate of a student's independent, instructional, and frustration levels in reading. The independent reading level refers to the level of difficulty which is low enough that the student can read alone with considerable ease. The instructional level is the level at which the student can learn as he or she reads. However, this level requires some assistance from the teacher. The frustration level is the reading level at which a student is unable to cope because the material is too difficult and causes the student to become frustrated. Having knowledge of these levels can assist the tutor in choosing appropriate reading materials for a student.

Informal reading inventories can be teacher-made. Most professional reading textbooks offer instructions for constructing informal reading inventories. Detailed instructions are given by Zintz (1981) in his text *Corrective Reading.* However, excellent informal reading inventories have been developed commercially and use of these can save the tutor time and energy. Some recommended commercially-prepared inventories include:

Ekwall, Eldon E. *Ekwall Reading Inventory.* 2nd ed. Boston: Allyn and Bacon, 1985.

Jacobs, H. Donald, and L.W. Searfoss. *Diagnostic Reading Inventory.* 2nd ed. Dubuque, Iowa: Kendall Hunt, 1979.

Silvaroli, Nicholas J. *Classroom Reading Inventory.* 5th ed. Dubuque, Iowa: William C. Brown, 1986.

Woods, Mary Lynn and Alden J. Moe. *Analytical Reading Inventory.* 3rd ed. Columbus, Ohio:

Charles E. Merrill, 1985.

Simplified Teacher-Made Inventories

Two teacher-made tests are discussed below. One is an oral reading grade level inventory. The second is a test for comprehension. Both procedures give approximations of appropriate reading levels, and they can give information concerning specific types of skills in which students need improvement.

The Oral Reading Grade Level Inventory. This assessment measure, adapted from Pope (1975), is one which can be used in conjunction with other diagnostic techniques to identify reading levels. In constructing this inventory, the tutor must secure a series of basal readers. One reader per level in the series beginning with the pre-primer level and continuing through the highest level in the series should be used. The tutor should mark off a sample reading passage of about 100 words near the end of each book. The student should begin reading at a level which is relatively easy for him or her. This is usually at least two grade levels below the student's actual grade level. If the student misses five or less words, he or she is required to continue reading the samples until six or more errors in 100 words are made.

Regarding reading levels, Pope notes that the book in which the student misses six or more words marks the frustration level. The highest grade level reader in which the student reads 95 words correctly out of a 100 word sample is the instructional level at which the student should be taught with basal materials. The level at which the student reads 98 percent of the words and understands at three-quarters of the main ideas is the student's independent reading level.

The oral reading test can also be used to identify various types of oral reading errors made by the student. The tutor should have a copy of the passages as the student reads and should make notations of specific errors made. Where it appears that certain types of errors are repeated, the tutor may wish to plan some activities to deal with the problems.

Strategies and codes such as the following may be useful to the tutor in noting certain types of errors:

1. Repetitions: Underline with a wavy line.

2. Omitted words or parts of words: Encircle.

3. Substitutions: Draw a line through the original word and write the substitution above.

4. Insertions: Mark insertions with a caret and write the added word(s) in the sentence.

5. Pause before words: Draw two vertical lines in the place where pause was taken.

6. Word pronounce by teacher: Pronounce word if hesitation is over five seconds and place the letter P above the word. (Do not count unknown proper names as errors.)

7. Punctuation: Write X in the place where punctuation is not observed.

The Silent Reading Inventory. This inventory is based on a series of graded passages or short stories. Here, the student must read each selection silently and respond to comprehension questions upon completion of each passage. The tutor must develop thoughtful questions for use in the inventory.

In developing questions for the selected passages, the tutor should include various types of questions. There should be higher level thinking questions as well as questions which require recall of factual information. Questions with "yes" or "no" answers should be avoided unless they are followed up by "why" or "how" questions. In constructing the reading inventory, it is good to label the questions according to type. Codes may be used for labeling as follows:

D or F   (Detail or Factual)

MI   (Main Idea)

I   (Inferential)

Tutors should record appropriate answers to questions before the inventory is administered. In this way, they will have acceptable answers in mind by which to judge students' answers. A tutor may query students to clarify ambiguous answers but should not provide any clues to the correct answers. For inventories which utilize graded silent reading selections, Pope (1975) advises that the level in which the student answers three quarters of the questions correctly be considered the instructional level.

The following paragraph and the related comprehension questions were prepared by the author. The exercise presents the type of questions that are appropriate for an informal reading inventory.

All insects hatch from eggs. They have lsegs that can bend and bodies that are divided into three parts. The three body parts are the head, the chest, and the abdomen. Insects have feelers called antennae and most have one or two pairs of wings. They also have an outside shell called a skeleton. Whether they are butterflies, moths, grasshoppers, or any other insects, they are all alike in many ways.

1. Name two animals that are insects. (D)

2. What are the three body parts that all insects have? (D)

3. What is the skeleton of an insect? (D)

4. Why are some animals insects? (MI)

5. What is another word for the feelers of an insect? (D)

6. What is the largest number of wings that one insect can have? (I)

7. Tell one thing that mother insects do? (I)

Word Recognition Tests

The *San Diego Quick Assessment* (LaPray and Ross, 1969) is a test that presents ten words at each grade level from preprimer through grade eleven. The test is easy to administer and can be completed in a short period of time. It is reported that there is a high degree of agreement between performance on the *San Diego Quick Assessment* and informal reading inventory results (Zintz, 1981). Instructions for administering the test may be found in:

La Pray, Margaret and Ramon Ross. "The Graded Word List: Quick Gauge of Reading of Ability," *Journal of Reading* 12 (January 1969), pp. 305-307.

The *Dolch Basic Sight Word Vocabulary*, discussed in Chapter 4, can also be used as a word recognition test. The 220 words in the list represent basic high frequency words that all children reading at the third grade level or above should be able to recognize as sight words. Details for using the list as a sight word test are given by Zintz (1981, pp. 67-75).

Word recognition tests offer some estimation of a student's reading ability. Given several times during a year, they can be used as one measure of progress.

They are not, however, reading achievement tests and should not be used for making serious decisions about a student's progress in reading. Some children may be skilled at word calling but have little understanding of word meaning and may lack good comprehension skills.

Phonics Tests

An excellent phonics survey is provided by Ekwall (1986, pp. 246-260) in *Teacher's Handbook on Diagnosis and Remediation in Reading*. The test, entitled the *El Paso Phonics Survey*, tests knowledge of initial consonants, consonant digraphs, consonant blends, vowels, diphthongs, and *r-, l-,* and *w-* controlled vowels. It also tests a student's knowledge of some commonly used vowel generalizations. Tests such as the *El Paso Phonics Survey* can be used when tutors wish to assess phonics knowledge by a measure that is more comprehensive than teacher-made materials and/or activities from textbooks and workbooks.

Other commercially-prepared phonics tests that tutors might find helpful are:

"Baumann Informal Phonics Test" in Baumann, James T. *Reading Assessment: An Instructional Decision-Making Perspective.* Columbus, Ohio: Merrill Publishing Company, 1988, pp. 307-312.

This test has three parts: "Consonant Letter/Sound Correspondences," "Vowel Letter/Sound Correspondences," and "Vowel Generalizations and Reversals."

Miller, Wilma H. in the *Reading Diagnosis Kit,* 2nd ed. West Nyack, New York: The Center for Applied Research in Education, 1978, pp. 230-233.

This kit provides phonics tests for readers who are at or beyond the upper primary reading level.

113

Other Word Recognition Skills Assessment Measures

In addition to the areas of assessment mentioned above, other word recognition skills can also be assessed through commercially developed tests and worksheets and through teacher-made materials. In the area of structural analysis, Ekwall (1986) has prepared one test for knowledge of syllable principles and another for knowledge of contractions. Heilman (1984) has devoted considerable attention to exercises suitable for both diagnostic and instructional purposes in the area of structural analysis. In conjunction with teacher-made materials, such activities can be very useful to those who tutor students in reading.

With regard to context clues Ekwall (1986) has developed a test that uses graded passages for grades one through six reading levels. For each level, a student can be rated as excellent, good, fair, or poor in terms of his or her ability to use the context for completing cloze type passages. In general, the cloze procedure, discussed in Chapter 5, relies on the use of context clues and is a sound tool for assessment purposes. The procedure can be helpful in measuring general understanding of written material, language facility, background knowledge, specialized vocabulary, and other competencies. Specific directions for using the cloze procedure and variations of this procedure as diagnostic tools are given Gillet and Temple (1986, pp. 157-161) in *Understanding Reading Problems.*

Observation as an Assessment Technique

Observing students and making notes of their strengths and weaknesses in reading can be a powerful assessment technique. Observation can be the basis for supporting or questioning the results of formal tests and other assessment measures. Once tutors have goals and objectives established for working with students, observations can assist in making needed adjustments in on-going instructional programs. It is important for tutors to constantly observe the behaviors of their students and to use the information obtained in planning for instruction.

The following checklists adapted from Rupley and Blair (1983, pp. 48-49) are representative of observation checklists that can assist tutors in focusing on the progress of their students in the major areas of reading.

Primary Grades Checklist

(+) = Mastery   (/) = Satisfactory

(-) = Needs Improvement

____Basic sight vocabulary

____Auditory discrimination of sounds

____Visual discrimination of letters

____Initial consonants

____Final consonants

____Consonant blends

____Consonant digraphs

____Long vowels

____Short vowels

____Vowel digraphs

____Vowel diphthongs

____Vowel principles

____Auditory perception of syllables

____Root words

____Contractions

____Compound words

____Syllabication principles

_____Affixes

_____Semantic clues

_____Syntactic clues

_____Recall of factual information

_____Ability to relate events in proper sequence

_____Ability to determine the main idea

_____Ability to infer meaning

Intermediate Grades Checklist

(+) = Mastery   (/) = Satisfactory

(-) = Needs Improvement

_____Basic sight vocabulary

_____Vowel digraphs

_____Vowel diphthongs

_____Vowel principles

_____Root words

_____Contractions

_____Compound words

_____Syllabication principles

_____Affixes

_____Semantic clues

_____Syntactic clues

_____Recall of factual information

_____Ability to determine the main idea

_____Ability to infer meaning

_____Ability to evaluate content

_____Flexibility of reading rate dependent on purpose and material

Summary

Tutors must make both initial and on-going efforts to obtain information about students' reading abilities. First of all, relevant background information should be obtained, including the assessment of classroom teachers and results of formal tests. Then, informal assessment by tutors is needed. Informal techniques such as the informal reading inventory and various assessment measures for word recognition skills can be very helpful.

BIBLIOGRAPHY

Chapter 6

Burns, Paul C., Betty D. Roe, and Elinor P. Ross. *Teaching Reading in Today's Elementary Schools.* 4th ed. Boston: Houghton Mifflin, 1988.

Ekwall, Eldon E. *Teacher's Handbook on Diagnosis and Remediation in Reading.* Boston: Allyn and Bacon, 1986.

Gillet, Jean W. and Charles Temples. *Understanding Reading Problems.* 2nd. ed. Boston: Little Brown and Company, 1986.

Heilman, Arthur W. *Phonics in Proper Perspective.* 5th ed. Columbus, Ohio: Charles E. Merrill, 1984.

La Pray, Margaret and Ramon Ross. "The Graded Word List: Quick Gauge of Reading Ability," *Journal of Reading* 12 (January 1969).

Pikulshi, John J. and Timothy Shanahan. *Approaches to the Informal Evaluation of Reading.* Newark, Delaware: International Reading Association, 1982.

Pope, Lillie. *Guidelines To Teaching Remedial Reading.* 2nd ed. New York: Book-Lab Inc., 1975.

Rauch, Sidney J. and Joseph Sanacore. *Handbook for the Volunteer Tutor.* Newark, Delaware: International Reading Association, 1985.

Richek, Margaret, Lynne K. List, and Janet W. Lerner. *Reading Problems: Assessment and Teaching Strategies.* 2nd ed. Englewood Cliffs, New Jersey: Prentice Hall, 1989.

Rupley, William H. and Timothy R. Blair. *Reading Diagnosis and Direct Instruction: A Guide for the*

Classroom. 2nd ed. New York: Houghton Mifflin, 1983.

Spache, George D. and Evelyn B. Spache. *Reading and the Elementary School.* Boston: Allyn and Bacon, 1986.

Zintz, Miles V. *Corrective Reading.* 4th ed. Dubuque, Iowa: William C. Brown, 1981.

INDEX